VISION-QUEST

VISION QUEST

A PERSONAL JOURNEY THROUGH MAGIC AND SHAMANISM

NEVILL DRURY

PRISM · UNITY

Originally published by Prism Press in 1984

This revised edition published in Great Britain in 1989 by

PRISM PRESS
2 South Street
Bridport
Dorset DT6 3NQ

and distributed in the USA by

AVERY PUBLISHING GROUP INC.
350 Thorens Avenue
Garden City Park
New York 11040

and published in Australia 1989 by

UNITY PRESS
6a Ortona Road
Lindfield
NSW 2070

1 85327 034 2

Printed and bound in the Channel Islands
by The Guernsey Press Limited

The Author

Nevill Drury was born in Hastings, England, in 1947 but has lived most of his life in Australia. He finds magical philosophy an inspiring area of pursuit and has made several national radio and television appearances in defence of 'occult' view-points.

   He has contributed numerous articles to periodicals and journals in the field and is the author of several books on western magic that have attracted international recognition. These include *Don Juan, Mescalito and Modern Magic*, *Inner Visions* and *The Shaman and the Magician*. He holds a Masters degree in anthropology and works as an acquisitions editor in the Australian publishing industry.

*For Ben, to whom these things
are a total mystery*

Preface and Acknowledgements

From an occult viewpoint, many people at different times have helped and influenced me. Among those whom I wish to thank especially are Stephen Skinner, Moses Aaron and Michael Harner, and the many other occultists with whom I have worked. Their encouragement and sense of ritual innovation in our ventures together have given rise to the magical journeys which are the basis of this book. Without them, very little could have been achieved.

I also wish to thank Catherine Colefax, Cheryl Weeks and Moses Aaron for permission to reproduce extracts from their magical records.

. . . we are carefully to proceed in Magick, lest that Syrens and other monsters deceive us, which likewise do desire the society of the humane soul. Let the Magician carefully hide himself alwaies under the wings of the most High, lest he offer himself to be devoured of the roaring Lion.

— *The Arbatel of Magick* (1655)

Contents

CHAPTER ONE

First Journey

For me, magic has always been an internal event, a process of discovering the richness and beauty of the symbols of the unconscious mind. Many people equate magic and occultism with theatrical robes and ceremonial, or with the type of trickery and visual deception presented as the wizardry of the conjuror. While it is true that some occultists, William Butler Yeats included, have found the use of magical regalia, symbolic adornments and rehearsed ritual drama within a temple to be stimulating and inspiring, I have not been drawn to that approach. For me, magic is a venture into the sacred realms of the unconscious mind and, like meditation, does not require external ceremony.

My first such encounter with the sacred mythology of magic took place in 1968 during my first involvement with LSD. I was certainly not anticipating the type of mystical experience that would, in a very substantial way, change my life.

I had taken 200 micrograms of LSD with a group of university friends. We were having a party and listening to a variety of rock albums including music by Vanilla Fudge and Jefferson Airplane. In Timothy Leary's sense, our 'set and setting' were excellent: mentally we were well attuned to each other and thoroughly enjoying each other's company. The party atmosphere was supportive and unthreatening. At the time I did not realise how crucial such factors would be when one enters an altered state of consciousness.

I recall that we passed a mango around the room and rejoiced at its extraordinary texture, and its special power as a sacramental offering. All of these things were events relating to our unity, activities symbolising our friendship. After a while it seemed that my energy level was changing. I leaned back against an armchair as an awesome array of pictures swept before my eyes. Meanwhile one of my friends, Stephen, who was well versed in esoteric literature, suggested to me that he might be able to guide me up the so-called 'middle pillar' of the Tree of Life, towards that inner level of centredness known in the Kabbalah as Tiphareth, where the ego becomes much less important and where a much more total sense of wellbeing dawns within the consciousness. I was broadly familiar with what he was proposing, but quite unaware of the technique. He began to read to me from a Rosicrucian book by the famous adept, the Comte de Saint Germain. The book is titled *The Most Holy Trinosophia* and is translated from a manuscript in the French library at Troyes. It contains a series of initiatory alchemical visions and had been prized by many occultists through history, including Count Allesandro Cagliostro. His copy of the work had been seized by members of the Inquisition in Rome in 1789. So here was I, unwittingly entering into an initiatory process using one of the strongest psychedelics available to modern man.

As I rested against the armchair, Stephen began to read to me from the *Trinosophia*. Meanwhile I began to participate in the visions themselves. No longer did they belong to the Rosicrucian world of the Comte de Saint Germain — they had become my own personal revelation.

In an early section of the *Trinosophia* the journey resembles the path that the mystical figure Aeneas takes to find the Golden Bough. In this text the magician descends through the volcano Vesuvius to the underworld:

The clouds gathered overhead. Lightning flashed through the night and gave to the flames of the volcano a bloodlike appearance. At last I arrived and found an iron altar where I

2

placed the mysterious bough . . . I pronounce the formidable words . . . instantly the earth trembles under my feet, thunder peals . . . The choirs of the genii rise in the air and make the echoes repeat the praises of the Creator . . . the hallowed bough which I had placed on a triangular altar suddenly is ablaze. A thick smoke envelopes me. I cease to see. Wrapped in darkness, I seemed to descend into an abyss. I know not how long I remained in that situation. When I opened my eyes I vainly looked for the objects which had surrounded me a little time ago. The altar, Vesuvius, the country around Naples, had vanished from my sight. I was in a vast cavern, alone, far away from the world.

I had begun my journey through the earth, at the base of the Tree of Life, and soon felt surrounded by goblins and fairy-folk, whose energies and activities seemed to be sustaining Nature and assisting the very processes of Life itself. I was now told that I would begin to travel towards the Moon, symbolically associated with the White Goddess, fertility and sexuality. A girl who had been sitting nearby came and sat behind me on the armchair, and placed her hands across my eyes. Spontaneously I reached down to hold her ankles, and this resulted in an extraordinary outburst of energy. A current of life-force flowed through me as if a new circuit had been connected. Meanwhile my journey was taking me towards the Goddess:

At last, after a long, long march I came to a square chamber. A door in the middle of each of its four sides opened; they were different colours and each door was placed at one of the four cardinal points. I entered through the north door which was black; the opposite one was red; the door to the east was blue and the one facing it was of dazzling white . . . In the middle of this chamber was a square mass; on its centre shone a crystal star. On the north side was a painting representing a woman naked to the waist; a black drapery fell over her knees and two silver bands adorned her garment. In her hand was a rod which she placed against the forehead of a man facing her across the table, which stood on a single support and bore a cup and a lance-head. A sudden flame rose from the ground . . .

3

While I know now that Yesod — the Kabbalistic centre of sexuality and the emotions — is traditionally associated with the Lunar Goddess, I was quite unaware of these psychic process at the time and the thinly veiled symbolism of rods and cups hadn't even occurred to me. Neither was there any sense of a sexual relationship with the girl who sat behind me on the armchair. Nevertheless, the energy that was bonding us was unquestionably sexual, similar perhaps to the energies of Tantric Yoga. I was surrounded by silver, lunar light, and for a time beseiged by 'lunatic' creatures that clustered all around me in fun. Then 'as the flame rose from the ground' I too found myself rising into the air. I was becoming light and airy. I seemed to have no bodily awareness whatever, almost like a mind devoid of any physical perspective. I began to soar, drawn up into a cloud of golden light. Then, from the middle of the light, I was aware of a sacred being coming towards me. Extraordinary radiance beamed from his body and the sense of wellbeing and peace was overwhelming. The sacred being, whom I can only describe as Christ-like, welcomed me to his domain, and for a period of time that seemed far beyond any finite measure I swam in an ocean of light. It was truly awesome and, for many days afterwards, totally beyond my powers of verbal communication. I later managed to thank my friends briefly for helping me towards such a profound experience but it wasn't possible at that time to relay to them its actual significance for me. Early the next morning I walked the two miles back to my house overwhelmed by what had occurred and totally lost in silence.

Later on, the experience began to pose questions for me that I found difficult to answer. I had not been raised in an orthodox Christian family — my religious perspectives were mainly influenced by Theosophy which my father and grand-mother adhered to — and yet the peak of my mystical experience had been predominantly Christian in tone. Was Christ one of several gods of light that universally symbolise spiritual awakening in different religious traditions? Could this sacred being also have been Osiris, Helios or Apollo? Why had a journey that had begun with a Kabbalistic and Rosicrucian emphasis and had been enhanced by LSD, culminated in such a 'Christian' way? I began to think that what we understand as Christ-consciousness is a universal state of being, and not at all restricted to one religion. But more than that, I began to marvel at the scope of esoteric states of consciousness. What secrets had these Rosicrucian adepts tapped? Where had they obtained their knowledge of occult symbols, and what exactly underlay the process of initiation? I did not realise at the time that these questions would take me many years to answer.

I began to read every serious work on magic and occult philosophy that I could lay my hands on, especially the writings of nineteenth-century occultist MacGregor Mathers, who had translated the Kabbalah from Latin into English, and Aleister Crowley, whose works were voluminous but often very absorbing. Although he had gained notoriety in the 1930s for his escapades as the 'Great Beast' his *Book of Thoth* was accompanied by the only visionary Tarot pack in existence. A.E. Waite's books were also essential, and his scholarship embraced Kabbalah, Rosicrucianism, Tarot and the Holy Grail legends. I was strongly recommended to read Dion Fortune's *The Mystical Qabalah* and Israel Regardie's *The Tree of Life*, widely considered to be among the best contemporary books on magical philosophy. Dion Fortune was both an occultist and a Jungian psychotherapist, and her book reflected the blend of mythology and psychology that seemed appropriate. Then there were the voluminous Order Papers of the Golden Dawn society to which many of these occultists had belonged. Israel Regardie had edited and released his four-volume compilation of Golden Dawn tracts through the Aries Press in Chicago in the late 1930s, but it was hard to find. I eventually tracked down a dog-eared set in an antiquarian bookshop.

Most of these occultists presented magic as an accumulation of all the philosophies and religions that had become heretical or had gone underground alongside the established Christian Church. I later read with interest the writings of numerous Gnostic sects and was intrigued by the wranglings between these groups and orthodox Christian leaders like Irenaeus and Tertullian, who wanted to make heretics of them. Then there were the medieval Kabbalists and alchemists like Paracelsus, Thomas Vaughan and Cornelius Agrippa who presented complex, esoteric views of man, and the works of Wallis Budge, whose translations of the *Egyptian Books of the Dead* and related tracts influenced many occult rituals incorporating Egyptian mythology.

There were also the tales of jealousy and power: Aleister Crowley's confrontation with William Butler Yeats in the Golden Dawn and his loathing for A.E. Waite, whom he regarded quite unjustly as ponderous and dull; the schisms that divided the late Golden Dawn society, and the despotism of MacGregor Mathers who demanded financial support from his followers while he translated occult classics at leisure in a Paris museum. It all seemed rather discouraging. I wondered why people whose inner task was so profound could get caught up in petty wrangles for power or for higher grades of initiation. Surely there was more to it than that?

Meanwhile I was drawn to the visionary writings and illustrations of a man who stood out as a unique and impressive occultist: Austin Osman Spare.

CHAPTER TWO

The Gods of Trance

My first contact with the works of Austin Spare was an article in the encyclopedic magazine *Man, Myth and Magic*. It was a brief description of the English visionary artist, written by his friend and fellow occultist Kenneth Grant. I was intrigued by how Spare seemed able to tap the creative powers of his unconscious mind by entering a trance state at will, and I was determined to find out more about him.

In 1971 I spent a considerable period in the British Museum, leafing through fragile, hand-bound volumes of Spare's privately published writings. I was working at the time at Bryce's Bookshop in Museum Street, just a few doors away from that famous arcane centre, the Atlantis Bookshop, and spent every available moment either in the Museum itself or combing the shelves in Atlantis for obscure volumes.

I discovered that Spare had begun as a relatively orthodox book illustrator, very much in the style of Edmund J. Sullivan, one of the principal interpreters of *Omar Khayyam*. Spare had won a scholarship to the Royal College of Art in Kensington when he was sixteen and was obviously highly regarded because Augustus John had admired his work. Spare had illustrated a collection of aphorisms titled *The Starlit Mire* and this had been published in 1911 by John Lane, a great supporter of ornate book illustration. Despite the representational style, however, the work was far from orthodox. A satyr was shown lurking in the folds of a lady's dress in the

An atavistic
illustration by
Austin Spare, from
The Starlit Mire (1911)
*Courtesy: Kenneth
Grant/Ada Millicent
Pain*

frontispiece to the book, and a line sketch of Spare himself
featured a decorative sculpture of Pan and his pipes. There was
obviously a strong pagan undercurrent in his work. One of the
most impressive drawings in *The Starlit Mire* depicted Spare in a
dream reverie, surrounded by horned animals and a primitive
horned man — a clear representation of the artist's fascination
for atavistic imagery. Among Spare's other works were *Earth
Inferno*, a book which parodied the human condition, *Focus of
Life*, which included some extraordinary pencil sketches of
sumptuous women surrounded by ethereal presences, and *A
Book of Satyrs* which contained visual 'satires' on priests,
doctors, prudes, socialites, bureaucrats and politicians. But
the most compelling of all of Spare's books was *The Book of
Pleasure*, first published in 1913 when the artist was only 27
years old. In this book Spare presented not only his finest

graphic illustrations but also the essence of his magical philosophy. Included were such works as 'The Instant of Obsession', 'Stealing the Fire from Heaven', 'The Self's Vision of Enlightenment' and 'The Dwellers at the Gates of Silent Memory'. Many of the figures were animal-human fusions and the mood was distinctly surreal and dream-like. Accompanying them were Spare's theories on trance states and details of his exploration of primeval states of conscious- ness, which he regarded as remnants of earlier incarnations.

Spare believed that the essence of magic lay in the powers of the will, and that an instruction to the subconscious mind could be focused by condensing the actual words of an instruction into a single symbol or 'sigil'. This sigil was rather like an anagram. In *The Book of Pleasure*, Spare gives the following example:

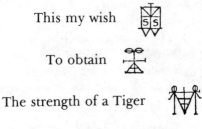

The secret of implanting the sigil into the unconscious lay in making the conscious mind blank at the time of the magical act. The peak of sexual orgasm was an ideal way of doing this, but states of exhaustion or self-hypnosis would also do. Spare himself practised a form of self-induced trance where he meditated on his reflection in a mirror until his body went rigid. He called this *The Death Posture*. The essential ingredient according to Spare was 'mental vacuity', the ultimate state of receptivity. The technique produced a type of psychic openness which could be used to produce automatic drawings.

In an article written with Frederick Carter for *Form* magazine (1916) Spare wrote:

> Automatic drawings can be obtained by such methods as concentrating on a *sigil* — by means of exhausting mind and body pleasantly in order to obtain a condition of non-consciousness . . . Drawings should be made by allowing the hand to run freely with the least possible deliberation. In time shapes will be found to evolve, suggesting conceptions, forms and ultimately having personal or individual style. The *mind in a state of oblivion*, without desire towards reflection or pursuit of materialistic intellectual suggestions, is in a condition to produce successful drawings of one's *personal* ideas, symbolic in meaning and wisdom.

Spare had a very specific idea of what he meant by 'personal'. For him the personality had evolved through many forms, animal as well as human, and it was in the trance state that images of past existences — *atavistic resurgences* — made themselves known by manifesting in visions and in art. Spare, who referred to himself in his writings by his magical name *Zos*, believed that he could retrace his earlier existences and, after locating his first personality, could transcend it and merge with the Void, which he called *Kia*. It was a type of Tibetan Buddhism in reverse, but it can be argued that Spare, somewhere along the line, got lost in the transcendental process. While his early work showed a beautiful artistic precision and subtlety of form, his later work, permeated by the astral imagery of trance experiences, became more diffuse and ill-defined.

It is important to point out that Spare was not only summoning images of creativity, but using his trance technique as a form of visionary magic. He was intrigued by the animal-headed deities of ancient Egypt, the very home of the arcane mysteries, and felt that such god-energies could be summoned from the unconscious:

> Their numerous Gods, all partly animal, bird, fish . . . prove the completeness of that knowledge. The cosmogony of their

A rare trance painting by Austin Spare, from his later period *Courtesy: Obelisk Gallery, London*

Gods is proof of their knowledge of the order of evolution, its complex processes from the one's simple organism . . . All Gods have lived (being ourselves) on earth, and when dead, their experience or Karma governs our actions in degree.

Spare was not the only one who had regarded the gods as being alive in the unconscious mind. The same concept is intrinsic to Carl Jung's theory of archetypes and also features strongly in the contemporary frameworks of consciousness put forward by scholars like David Miller and James Hillman. But Spare was deriving these views from his own visionary experiences. He had learnt his trance technique from a witch named Mrs Paterson, who claimed a psychic connection with the witches of Salem, and he also produced automatic drawings in trance through the mediumship of an American Indian spirit entity called Black Eagle, whom Spare claimed to see on several occasions.

11

By comparison with most of the other occult figures my research was turning up, Austin Spare was quite remarkable. However although I admired his originality, there were elements in his work that disturbed me greatly. For one thing, he seemed to be uncovering very primeval aspects of consciousness — one could almost say bestial aspects — and I tended to doubt the value of plunging into a psychic current which ran counter to normal evolutionary processes. More importantly, by contrast with shamanism — a technique where the magician endeavours to control the trance state — Spare had become a type of artistic medium, where such controls were not inherent. Mediumism allows more spontaneous content to come through from the unconscious mind but in my view there is a much greater chance of mental derangement as a result.

So to some extent Spare's magical techniques, for me, were a dead-end, but nevertheless highly instructive. While I admired Spare's sense of psychic adventure in 'stealing the fire from heaven' I did not feel inclined to try to emulate him in that way. Even so, I felt that Spare's work was unique and deserved recognition. It had not been described at any length in any existing occult publications*. So I presented my essay on Spare to occult publisher Neville Armstrong, who had his offices near to the Museum in Whitfield Street. Armstrong undertook to track down further works by the artist that had been displayed in the Obelisk Gallery and these were published in the book which grew out of my research on Spare, *The Search for Abraxas*.

For me a sort of occult adventure was beginning, and part of it had to do with the symbolism of the Gnostic god Abraxas,

---

* Kenneth Grant's biography *Images and Oracles of Austin Osman* was not published until 1975 and the lengthy article on him in the occult magazine *Agapé* did not appear until 1973.

whom I had chosen as a focus for the book. This is a story in itself, and the symbolism of Abraxas was to recur later in the shamanic work in very surprising ways.

I first read about Abraxas in Jung's *Septem Sermones Ad Mortuos* (Seven Sermons to the Dead). Jung had written this work in extraordinary circumstances and had elevated Abraxas to the level of a supreme God, encompassing both good and evil. The book has a profoundly inspirational quality and arose as an example of automatic writing from the depths of Jung's unconscious. In his autobiography *Memories, Dreams, Reflections*, Jung recalls that the book came about at a time when he was resolving a tension between the outer world of his professional and family life, and the inner world of his imagination. For a while he felt possessed:

> Very gradually the outlines of an inner change began to make their appearance within me. In 1916 I felt an urge to give shape to something. I was compelled from within, as it were, to formulate and express what might have been said by Philemon.*
> This was how *Septem Sermones Ad Mortuos* with its peculiar language came into being . . . It began with a restlessness, but I did not know what it meant or what 'they' wanted of me. There was an ominous atmosphere all around me . . . The whole house was filled as if there were a crowd present, crammed full of spirits. They were packed deep right up to the door and the air was so thick it was scarcely possible to breathe. As for myself I was all a-quiver with the question: 'For God's sake, what in the world is this? Then they cried out in chorus 'We have come back from Jerusalem where we found not what we sought'. That is the beginning of the *Septem Sermones*. Then it began to flow out of me, and in the course of three evenings the thing was written. As soon as I took up the pen the whole ghostly assemblage evaporated. The room quieted and the atmosphere cleared. The haunting was over.

---

* Jung regarded Philemon as a mysterious, sage-like entity within his own unconscious, 'almost a living personality'. He had first seen Philemon in a dream, when he appeared as an old man with the horns of a bull and the wings of a kingfisher, sailing across the sky.

Jung ascribed the work to 'Basilides in Alexandria, the city where the East toucheth the West'. He clearly believed that Philemon was some sort of Gnostic or pagan persona operating at a profound level in his unconscious. Abraxas is mentioned in several of the Sermons and is described in various ways:

'This is a god whom ye knew not, for mankind forgot it. We name it by its name Abraxas . . . Abraxas standeth above the sun and above the devil'. (Sermo II)

'Abraxas (provides) Life, altogether indefinite, the mother of good and evil . . . The power of Abraxas is two fold . . . Abraxas begetteth truth and lying, good and evil, light and darkness, in the same word and in the same act'. (Sermo III)

'Between man and his one god there standeth nothing, so long as man can turn away his eyes from the flaming spectacle of Abraxas'. (Sermo VII)

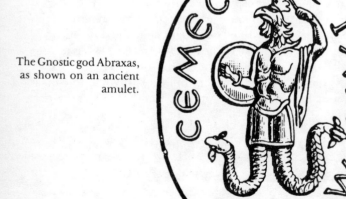

The Gnostic god Abraxas, as shown on an ancient amulet.

Jung circulated the text of *Septem Sermones* among a few friends in 1916 but it was little known until 1925, when it was privately published. It is likely that Hermann Hesse drew on Jung's work for his superb magical novel *Demian*, in which there are further details of Abraxas. The central character, Emil Sinclair, is told by the eccentric musician Pistorius: 'Our god . . . is called Abraxas, and he is both god and devil; he contains in himself the world of light and the world of darkness. Abraxas has nothing to object to in any of your thoughts or any of your dreams. Always remember that. But once you become faultless and normal he abandons you in favour of a new vessel into which he can pour his thoughts'. Elsewhere Hesse went on to expand the Gnostic cosmology: 'The bird is struggling out of the egg. The egg is the world. Whoever wants to be born must first destroy a world. The bird is flying to God. The name of the God Is Abraxas'.

Here, within the writings of Jung and Hesse, a very profound and mysterious entity had presented itself, a deity that symbolised trancendence of both good and evil and that, for me, presented the polarity of human consciousness and aspiration that I felt to be very important. As I had already discovered, magical philosophy portrayed good and evil very clearly as opposite modes of being that needed to be equally heeded; I often had the impression that Christianity and other major religions were inclined to downplay the reality of evil in favour of the overriding aim of spiritual redemption. Here, in the form of the Gnostic deity Abraxas, the principle of dynamic balance was being clearly addressed. The mystical venture into the sacred depths of the unconscious, among the awesome images of both chaos and transcendence, was strongly evoked by Jung's presentation of Abraxas.

However, I soon discovered that tracing the historical origins of Abraxas was no easy task. Many of the Gnostic teachings were known mainly through the writings of Irenaeus, the Christian bishop of Lyons (c. 180 A.D.), and Irenaeus was understandably hostile to the Gnostic heresies. Many amulets and talismans bearing the symbolism of Abraxas appeared in this period and characteristically showed the deity with a bird's head, human body and the legs of serpents. The value of the Greek letters of Abraxas had a numerical value of 365 and because he therefore symbolised the Year, the Gnostic god was popularly regarded as a ruler of day to day affairs — almost a deity of the horoscope. This view was promulgated by Irenaeus who wrote of Basilides and his followers: 'They distribute the positions of the 365 heavens as astrologers do . . . their first principle is Abraxas.'

It remains unclear how Basilides really regarded Abraxas. Abraxas has been linked to the Greek lion-headed god called Aeon, the Iranian god of Time, Zurvan, and the Indian sky-god Varuna. The Gnostic *Nag Hammadi Library* presents him as a 'great light' or 'keeper of the immortal soul', but not as a universal high-god.* So one is inevitably faced with conflicting views of Abraxas, some of them portraying him as a spiritual force, others as an astrological image on talismans valued mainly by the superstitious.

While we were developing the manuscript of *The Search for Abraxas* as an outline of the magical revival, it seemed to me and to my co-author Stephen Skinner, that the mythological Abraxas presented by Jung was a powerful and appropriate image. There are two great paths in Western Magic: the right and left-hand ascent of the Tree of Life, one embracing the holy archetypes, the other their demonic equivalents. According to the Kabbalah, these two paths finally meet in *Ain Soph Aur*, the limitless light that transcends both good and evil. So Abraxas, more than any other deity, was an ideal representation of the magical quest itself.

After a strange beginning, I was finding that my path into

---

* See the three books from the *Nag Hammadi Library*, *The Apocalypse of Adam*, *The Gospel of the Egyptians* and *Zostrianos*.

visionary forms of magic was well under way. Although Austin Spare and Carl Jung had vastly different approaches to their own psychic forces, both had tapped the extraordinary creativity latent in the unconscious and had become vehicles for its expression. Both had experienced first hand the mythology of the soul laid bare, and both had come to the conclusion that esoteric cosmologies — the ancient gods, whether of the Gnostic sects or the sun-worshipping Egyptians — were not merely mystical concepts from an era long past, but an ongoing reality that could be tapped in an altered state of consciousness. The thought of contacting these sacred areas of the mind was remarkable enough, but I also felt a need to do further study. What areas of mystical and magical experience, for example, were being explored in contemporary mind and consciousness research?

18

CHAPTER THREE

Pathways of the Mind

I was surprised to discover that there had been very little overlap between occultists and those who were part of the Human Potential Movement. The latter was, and is, a diverse group of people, mostly made up of psychologists but also including anthropologists, physicists, theologians, musicians, pharmacologists and philosophers, who were interested in the furthest reaches of human consciousness. Although one could justifiably assume that psychology *ought* to be all about the study of consciousness, this had not been the case since the time of William James. Since his day, psychology had gone off on a behaviourist tack and had veered away from the study of what actually makes us conscious. Perhaps human consciousness studying *itself* could never be regarded as sufficiently scientific or impartial.

The home of the Human Potential Movement for many years has been the Esalen Institute located in very picturesque countryside in the Big Sur, south of Monterey. These days the workshops on 'spiritual psychology' are far-ranging, and include a wide variety of bodywork therapies, polarity balancing, Tai Chi, Zen, creative sexuality, dance, hypnosis, shamanism, Taoism and special lectures on topics like the Gnostics and Findhorn. The present scholar-in-residence, Czechoslavakian psychiatrist Stanislav Grof, has also been president of the International Association of Transpersonal Psychology, a movement which grew out of Humanistic

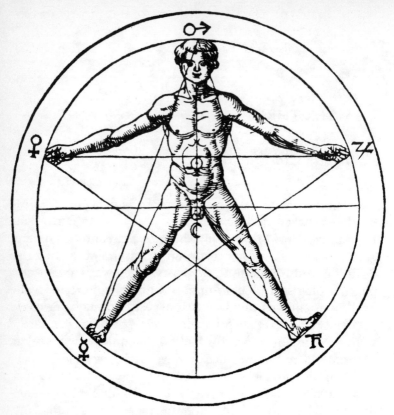

Psychology and which encourages research into visionary consciousness, peak-experiences and mysticism, in addition to all forms of wellbeing and holistic health. Transpersonal psychology had grown out of its Humanistic predecessor as a result of the very considerable efforts of Anthony Sutich and Abraham Maslow in the late 1960s and its growth as a school of psychology has paralleled the emergence of the Human Potential Movement. In Maslow's view, psychology had been far too dominated by the study of pathology and neurosis and not sufficiently involved with those states of supreme wellbeing that we all strive after. Maslow had also gone on record stating that religious values and mystical experience were a vital part of the human make-up, and deserved scientific study.

Since magic also had the aim of putting man in touch with his sacred origins, why, I wondered, had there been such little interchange between students of the Western Mystery Tradition and their 'higher consciousness' brothers and sisters in California? The one exception in the literature was an essay on western magic by William Gray in Charles Tart's anthology *Transpersonal Psychologies*, but apart from that there had obviously been very scant sharing of information. I still don't know the reason why.

One of the areas where there was potentially a certain amount in common was so-called 'active imagination' work. The occultists in the Golden Dawn had made extensive inner journeys of the mind by focusing on Tarot cards and the Hindu Tattva symbols of the four elements and had thereby learned to trigger controlled self-hypnosis states at will. Although Ralph Metzner had published a book called *Maps of Consciousness* which included descriptive chapters on the Tarot and alchemy, the only 'experiential' book I could find to throw light on these inner processes of visualisation was *Mind Games*, a book of guided imagery exercises. Its authors were Robert Masters and Jean Houston, Directors of the Foundation for Mind Research in Pomona, New York.

Mind Games presents a series of graded exercises in which members of a small group are guided by a leader into sensory areas of the imagination. Typically the early games begin with a relaxation exercise and lead progressively into areas which involve focusing, for example, on the body-image or on the sensory qualities of music. The games then progress to more complex visualisations where the participants imagine complete scenes — often of a mythic or fantasy nature — and learn to transfer consciousness to them, so that in an experiential sense they become real. Members of the group gradually learn to move in and out of the trance state at will, and to have encounters with sacred beings and the 'Group

Spirit'. The final sections of the book lead the participants through deep self-examination and towards the exploration of spiritual values, culminating in the experience of the quest for the Holy Grail and symbolic death and rebirth.

I could see the occult applications of these mind game techniques and resolved to make contact with the authors. Finally I managed to combine a professional publishing visit to New York with a journey to their home, located just outside the rural town of Suffern. Jean Houston was on a lecture-tour at the time but she later told me that her husband Robert was much more inclined towards mysticism and the occult than she was. And there was evidence of this in the environment they had created within their home. Located in lush, wooded countryside, the house was richly decorated with paintings, ornaments and wall-hangings that made it into a mythological event in its own right: a fur mandala from Greece hung on one wall, several Huichol peyote paintings on another. In Masters' study there were two authentic sculptures of the Egyptian lion-hearted goddess Sekhmet, one of which had an extra-ordinary psychic presence and seemed to follow you with its eyes around the room. I wasn't alone in this impression. Apparently anthropologist Margaret Mead had had the same feeling when she saw the sculpture, and had been very disturbed by it!

To my surprise I found that Robert Masters had moved on from the *Mind Games* work and was now much more specifically involved with the symbolism of Sekhmet and in linking mind research with the ancient Egyptian mysteries. He gave me a copy of his article *The Way of the Five Bodies*, which is an extraordinary statement of magical purpose expressed within the framework of Egyptian mythology. For Masters the only true spiritual transformations involve the two most subtle bodies of man, known by the Egyptians as *Khu* — the magical body — and *Sahu* the spiritual body.* When these are

---

* The other three bodies are *Aufu*, the physical body, *Ka*, the double, and *Haidit* the so-called 'shadow'.

fully operative the magician interacts with the gods and goddesses of the highest planes of being and becomes a participant in 'the war within the heavens'. In such an instance life is lived on a profound, cosmic level, far transcending ordinary reality. For Masters, the polar opposites are symbolised on the one hand by Sekhmet and her associated deities representing the forces of Light and Cosmos, and on the other by the dark god Set and his cohorts of Evil and Chaos. The most profound magical work results in sacred knowledge and self-realisation being conveyed to the occultist in a visionary state, directly by the god — in Masters' case, through Sekhmet.

This was impressive material, and far more grounded in occult mythology than I had expected from reading *Mind Games*, which is not aligned to a particular metaphysical system. In Masters' view a type of spiritual energy arousal was produced by his personal communication with Sekhmet, which paralleled the Yogic *Kundalini*. Although we did not discuss intimate details of the actual process for arousing this energy, the symbolism of Sekhmet (or Sekhet as she is sometimes known) is instructive. The husband of Ptah in the cosmology of Memphis, Sekhmet was regarded as guardian of the sun god and was also the Eye of Ra, whose energy she radiated forth. Kenneth Grant, an occultist working in the Tantric tradition, describes Sekhmet as 'the lion-headed goddess of the South; the type of solar-phallic or sexual heat . . . considered by the ancients as the divine inspirer or breather, the spirit of creation. Sekhet gave her name to the Indian concept of Sakti or Shakti, the creative power of Shiva . . . ' So Sekhmet/Sekhet has many of the qualities which are universally symbolised as typifying the magical quest: a force or spirit underlying creativity and a unique blending of polarities — a feminine bodily form, coupled with the lion's head and the 'fire of life' traditionally associated with male deities. Androgynous gods, those which depict the fusion of male and female in one form, have mythologically been regarded as the highest gods of all. The process of spiritual transformation in the Kabbalah similarly leads the magician beyond male and female polarities to the 'high neutrality' of *Kether*, the Crown — the peak of the Tree of Life and doorway to the infinte light *Ain Soph Aur.**

At the time of my meeting with Robert Masters, it is fair to say that I was not yet ready to embrace such a highly specific magical systems as that presented by the Sekhmet cosmology. Although my more recent work with shamanism has now led me towards similar conclusions regarding the aims of magic — which in the final analysis involves powerful interaction with the sacred archetypal gods of the subconscious — I was still at that time interested in specific active imagination techniques like those presented in *Mind Games*. One of my aims was to construct a complete system of visualisation pathways based on the Kabbalah and the Tarot — the magical systems most familiar to me.

There was also another topic on which I sought Robert Masters' opinion: the controlled use of psychedelics. I was aware that he and Jean Houston had spent fifteen years researching non-addictive psychedelics and had compiled one of the classical texts on LSD, *The Varieties of Psychedelic Experience*. They had also written the superbly visual, but long out-of-print *Psychedelic Art*, which I had finally managed to track down in a secondhand bookstore in Berkeley. I was particularly keen to have Masters' views on certain specific drug-states because I knew that Aleister Crowley had experimented with a variety of hallucinogens and had endeavoured to incorporate the resulting altered states of consciousness into his magical rituals. I was also aware that there was still considerable interest in psychedelics at Esalen, despite the legal constrictions. Stanislav Grof had researched the psychotherapeutic applications of LSD for nearly twenty

---

* For details of male and female polarities in the Major Arcana of the Tarot, readers are referred to my earlier book *Inner Visions*. The androgynous cards are also discussed.

years and when I first visited Esalen in 1979 I discovered that several members of staff were very intrigued by the potential applications of ketamine hydrochloride, a dissociative anesthetic that caused out-of-the-body experiences. John Lilly had also begun using ketamine extensively, and had written about it enthusiastically in his book *The Scientist.*

Robert Masters obviously still valued the insights that psychedelics could provide but cautioned me against the use of ketamine although he hadn't tried it himself. I told him about an article I had read by Grof's protege Rick Tarnas, who believed that ketamine had an extremely safe medical record and was virtually guaranteed to produce mystical states of consciousness. It seemed too good to be true. Masters was not convinced, and felt that the drug could possibly anesthetise the breathing apparatus unless used with extreme care.

So I put aside the question of the magical use of psychedelics. When I returned to Sydney I found that nobody I knew had any knowledge of ketamine at all, let alone whether it had magical applications or not. In the meantime I decided to stick to mind games and to construct a series of visualisations that could be used to tap archetypal and mythological areas of consciousness. My starting point was the Major Arcana of the Tarot.

Intrigued by the visual beauty of the Tarot, I had already begun researching the symbolism of the cards in the early 1970s. A spate of decks had flooded the market in response to the demands of the counter-culture, but the best-known Tarot pack was still the comparatively dull Rider Pack designed by A.E. Waite and Pamela Colman Smith. By contrast, the visionary pack of Aleister Crowley and Frieda Harris came as a revelation, although it was clear that Crowley had incorporated some of his own mythological ideas into the card sequence.*

---

* For example, he replaced *Strength* with *Lust* in deference to the Whore of Babalon, and replaced *The Emperor* with *The Star* — both personal aberrations.

I knew that Tarot cards were linked in the popular mind to gypsy fortune-telling but learned that they had been present in Italy a century before the gypsies arrived there — so the origin of the Tarot remained a genuine mystery. Some people claimed that the Tarot originated in ancient Egypt, among them French theologian Antoine Court de Gebelin, author of one of the early books on the subject, *Le Monde Primitif*. De Gebelin had encouraged these fanciful theories by claiming that the Tarot was part of an initiatory procedure in the Great Pyramid. However the medieval nature of the cards — which included all the symbols of chivalry and armoured knights — clearly discounted this theory. De Gebelin's view was typical of the romantic obsession with lost cultures. Many people interested in occult origins have looked back to a golden age which possessed a secret esoteric wisdom and have located the source of this wisdom in various countries, including ancient Egypt and the legendary 'lost continents' Atlantis and Lemuria.

But even if de Gebelin's theories concerning the historical origins of the Tarot seemed dubious, his view on the initiatory application of the Tarot struck a powerful chord with me. There did seem to be a pattern of spiritual growth in the cards, especially in the twenty-two mythological trumps of the Major Arcana.

I found as I read further that the French occultist Eliphas Levi had been responsible for combining the Major Arcana and the Kabbalistic Tree of Life and that for the first time this presented the Tarot cards as potential pathways into the mythological areas of the mind. This eccentric blend of esoteric symbols, subsequently decried by orthodox Kabbalistic scholars like Gershom Scholem, was taken up as a working system by the occultists in the Order of the Golden Dawn, and has since become central to western magic.

Having already had the experience of ascending the Middle Pillar during my LSD adventure, I felt that the Tree of Life was a good place to start. I began to analyse the symbolism of the

26

Major Arcana starting with the entry card of *The World* and culminating with the paradoxical symbol of *The Fool*. By 1974, when I assembled my notes for an article titled *The Inner Mythology*, my sequence on the Tarot looked something like this:

The World   This card represents the descent into the underworld of the subconscious. The dancer is reminiscent of Persephone, symbolising the perpetual cycle of the harvest, and therefore life and death. She is also androgynous — her genitals are hidden — and she represents both male and female, despite her apparent feminity.

Judgement   The figures rise from death towards the new life and light of the magical quest. They are

Judgement

27

shown gesturing with their arms to form the word L.V.X. . . . A new personality, a magical identity has to be formed. Hephaestos, the blacksmith is ascribed to this path . . . he is like the great shaman who forges a new identity for his magical candidates in trance.

The Moon	This card is also evolutionary: the lobster emerges from the waters; the wild dog becomes tame and less aggressive. The tides of life are cyclic.
The Sun	The young naked twins dancing show a sense of innocence, and the synthesis of sexual opposites. The magic mountain is still far off in the distance.
The Star	The White Goddess kneels beside a pool of water, the river of consciousness towards which the magician slowly makes his way. The card symbolises intuition and fertility, and the cup is reminiscent of the Holy Grail . . .
The Tower	The Tower of Babel — an arrogant attempt by man to scale the heights of heaven. *The Tower* is also the body, and a thunderbolt of divine energy — the lightning flash — would be devastating and harmful to the occultist who was not inwardly prepared. A hint here of the Kundalini power?
The Devil	Man and woman bound in chains, still trapped by their lower, bestial and materialistic nature. A card which reminds us all of our limited frameworks and the need for transformation.
Death	The skeleton slayer strides across the horizon. Death and carnage are everywhere, but death

The Star

leads to new life. The river of consciousness flows into the sun in the distance ... and actually leads to *Tiphareth*, at the centre of the Tree of Life.

Temperance   A wonderful card. The union of opposites, male and female, and the four elements all blended together. All the aspects of the lower subconscious find unity on this path. Tiphareth, the level of God-in-Man, is within reach.

The Hermit   The Hermit is like the Ancient of Days, rising above Time and wending his way up the magic mountain, following the lantern of his own inner light. For the first time on the journey, the inner qualities take priority over

29

outer ones. His outer persona is limited, for he is hidden in his cloak.

Justice	A path demanding balance, adjustment and total impartiality. The love of Venus combined with the stern justice of Mars. Here the mystic encounters his accumulated wrongdoing — his *karma*, if you like. Only truth can be admitted in the Hall of Justice. Reminiscent of Maat in Egyptian religion.
The Hanged Man	At first glance a man upside down, perhaps even a parody of Christ. On a deeper level, a reflection of a great mystery. In Crowley's pack, his head is a beacon, showing that he transmits light from a more profound source.
The Wheel of Fortune	The Tarot's form of the mandala — universal cycles of fate and destiny. An essentially neutral card; the magician must learn to transcend opposites as the wheel turns from feminine to masculine and back again.
Strength	The intuitive woman overcoming the brute strength of the lower animal nature. Complete mastery over the earlier stages of evolution; opening the mouth, or pathway, to a more universal consciousness.
The Charioteer	The reflector of truth, the eye of the heavens . . . a very mobile form of the guardian god. A form of Mars but ruled by the love and spirit of the Great Mother.
The Lovers	Another card bringing the polarities of male and female together. The twins of *The Sun* in a more spiritually evolved state of being. A wonderful path flowing out of the harmony of *Tiphareth*. Innocence regained.

The Charioteer

The Hierophant	A reminder that the priest is one who channels divine inspiration to the gathered congregation. A blend of wisdom and mercy.
The Emperor	Another form of the Great Father, more stationary than the Charioteer, and seated on a rock-hewn throne, overlooking the manifest world below. The Tarot's version of Zeus . . .
The Empress	The Great Mother, warm and beneficient. The Mother of all things, which flow from her womb to the finite world of forms. The partner in Life of the Great Father. Surrounded by wheat, she is also the mother of Persephone, whom we met on the first path . . .

The High Priestess	The Great Goddess but in a colder, more aloof aspect. She is virginal, and doesn't yet know man. Mythologically, her virginity is symbolic of purity.
The Magus	The virginal Male God, again pure and unsullied. He reaches upwards to the supreme mysteries but has not yet combined with the Great Goddess to produce the manifested universe. Linked to Thoth, the word and rhythm sustaining the Universe.
The Fool	The supreme paradox: he-who-knows-nothing. He who therefore knows that which is beyond everything — the unmanifested world of pure spirit. The Fool stands on the peak of the magic mountain; spirit and infinity are all around him. The Fool embraces that-which-is-not.

There seemed no doubt to me that the Tarot contained all the ingredients of a total initiatory system. The lowest card on the Tree, *The World*, led directly into the unconscious mind, and resembled the classical tales of descent into the underworld. Then the cards began to form clusters around the lunar and solar archetypes. *The Star*, *The Moon* and *The Sun* were good examples of these, but it was interesting that on the pathway of *The Sun* the children were presented as still very young, and not yet spiritually mature.

Around the centre of the Tree were Tarot paths which forced a person through a process of rigorous self-assessment and an honest encounter with all the follies of the ego — *The Devil*, *The Tower* and *Justice*, while in the form of *Death* it was clear that all of these illusions and vanities had to be destroyed prior to the experience of spiritual rebirth. *Temperance*, with its fusion of the four alchemical elements, was a superb example of harmony, as was *The Wheel of Fortune* located nearby.

The paths leading upwards from Tiphareth at the centre of the Tree were also symbolically appropriate: *The Lovers*, showing the gradual blending of sexual opposites (a theme also found in Yoga) and *The Hermit* in which the magician's personality was clearly less important than the spiritual quest itself. *The Hanged Man*, which in fact portrayed the reflection of spiritual light from above, similarly pointed the way to more sacred domains of consciousness.

The remainder of the cards were primarily refelctions of the great Male and Female archetypes, either in their dynamic forms (*The Charioteer, Strength*) or more static and regal counterparts (*The Emperor, The Hierophant, The Empress*). Virginity was also presented as a mythic form of purity, symbolic of very sacred pathways of consciousness, and here *The Magus* and *The High Priestess* were particularly appropriate. And the final pathway, paradoxically titled *The Fool*, was one of the most interesting of all. Here the individual was seen yielding totally to the cosmic spirit, surrendering all personal possessions and stepping from the cliff-edge of finite existence into the ocean of infinite light.

I was convinced that the Tarot needed to be presented as a meditative journey of the spirit. Most books on the Tarot were either heavily laden with obscure symbolism or else focused on the fortune-telling aspects which, from my point of view, had become quite a minor consideration. The actual processes of spiritual growth portrayed in the Major Arcana seemed comparatively straightforward but, as always in the occult, the central themes had become clouded by metaphysical details — a problem that one also finds with the Kabbalah. The answer seemed to lie in adapting the Major Arcana into a system of meditations and visualisations comparable to the guided imagery of Masters' and Houston's *Mind Games*.

I undertook the project with great enthusiasm.

CHAPTER FOUR

The Tarot and Beyond

The first Tarot meditations that I produced in this style were simple in the extreme. Here are some examples:

The World

Tides of energy are all around us, for we are in the presence of the sacred maiden of the earth. Her pure face is filled with sunlight which nourishes the leaves and flowers in the deep, abundant valley, and her flowing hair is the colour of golden wheat.

In her eyes are the reflections of the moon, for she will lead us into the twilight world beneath the earth and beyond the sky, where her dark sister rules the land of shadows.

But while she is with us now, Persephone is like a beacon. In her movements are rays of enrichment and warmth, and her radiant hair glistens like the newly risen sun across the fields.

She is the first path.

She is the entry to the world beyond time.

She is the Maiden of the World.

The Star

In the night sky a golden star glows with crystal light. The maiden of the stream guards the life-essence which she captures from the sun with her flask. Shimmering light flows through her body like a translucent vessel as she pours the waters of life into a pool below, and suddenly the earth all around her springs to life with new possibilities. She tells us that we too can transmit the light, heralding new hope and new abundance.

She is the fifth path.

She is the mediator between the golden star and earth.

She is the Star Maiden of the Life Stream.

Temperance

Before us stands the angel of day and night, guardian of the sun and moon, and master of the four elements which unite the whole universe in the magic cauldron. Here in the womb of the world, man can be born again from the ashes, and arise phoenix-like in quest of the inner sun.

We enter the flux, allowing ourselves to be refashioned after the manner of the gods, encompassing the cycles of life, death and rebirth, and journeying by night and day along the universal road.

Temperance shows us the elixir of new life, the magical Philosopher's Stone.

Temperance is the ninth path.

Guardian of new life and ruler of the four elements of the Universe.

The Emperor

Amidst the textured rocks of the timeless mountains sits the throned ruler of the Universe. He is awesome and all-knowing, yet merciful and just. His crown is of light and his vestments are fashioned from the fabric of the Universe. He presides over life in all its forms; his domain is illumined by fire, kindled by the Sun of Sacred Knowledge.

The Emperor sits vigilantly, ever-patient upon his throne, surveying the world of man. From his vantage point he looks out, ever-watchful for imbalance. He shows us the flux of life and death which sustains the Universe in an ageless cycle.

He is the eighteenth path.

He is the Monarch of the Universe.

The timeless and ever-present Ancient of Days.

Contemporary Tarot image
of *The Emperor*, by Wolfgang
Grasse
Courtesy of the artist

I still felt, though, that the aspect that I most wanted to
include, that of the magical journey itself, was missing. Finally
I undertook the lengthy task of presenting the complete
Major Arcana as a continuous sequence. I was also interested
in combining the magical visualisations with electronic
music, and found such records as Fripp and Eno's *Evening
Star*, Tangerine Dream's *Rubycon* and *Zeit*, Edgar Froese's
Epsilon in Malaysian Pale and several albums by Klaus Schulze,
including *Mirage* and *Moondawn*, to be especially useful. The
haunting vocal effects on the film soundtrack of *2001*,
'Requiem' and 'Lux Aeterna', also had an appropriate
magical quality.*

* The text of the 22-path Tarot journey is included under the heading 'The
Book of Visions' in my book *Don Juan, Mescalito and Modern Magic*. For more
details on combining electronic music and magical visualisations see
Appendix A in this book.

In practical terms, however, I soon discovered that a journey through the 22 pathways of the Tarot was far too demanding for most people, including occultists experienced in visualisation and relaxation techniques. I therefore decided to condense the journey into the essential initiatory pathway that had formed the magical focus of the Golden Dawn — the Middle Pillar ascent to Tiphareth at the centre of the Tree of Life. I have found this guided visualisation to be excellent in group-work, following a basic relaxation exercise, and I use a tape which combines 'Crystal Lake' from Klaus Schulze's *Mirage* and 'Maroubra Bay' from Edgar Froese's *Epsilon in Malaysian Pale* to establish the mystical setting. The following is the complete text of the magical visualisation, which is read to the group while the music plays:

> We find ourselves in a field of grass, with the wind blowing gently and birds whistling in the distance. We are at peace with the environment and feel the sun warming our skin. Nature's rhythms and life-forces flow through us.
>
> As we walk through the field we see looming before us a rocky cliff-face, hard and worn with time. The granite textures seem ageless, and there are rifts and channels like wrinkles upon the face of an old man. Suddenly these fissures in the rock deepen and an opening appears in the cliff, becoming a doorway. We pass into the rock, through the space that leads down between the worlds into the land beyond time itself.
>
> Before we entered the rock it was warm and bright. Now we are entering a world that is dark, damp and cool. And yet, despite the fact that we are in an unfamiliar domain, the earth welcomes us. All around us, forces and powers are at work, sustaining living things growing in the soil, and in the rock streams, and in the sun-filled air above.
>
> As we continue, we detect an ethereal glow at the end of the path. A misty greeny-brown light plays on the walls of the cave, and we see for the first time, as our vision grows clearer, that in the flecks of light-energy a figure is dancing.
>
> She is naked and youthful in appearance and yet, as we watch, her body takes different forms. As if in a mirror, we see

38

in her the fields of ripened wheat, and a golden light shines from her face. Then she darkens, hardening into rock. Waters now seem to flow over her form, dissolving its hardness, and she resembles the currents and eddies of a country stream carrying the grains of sand in their flow. A soft breeze rustles through her golden hair.

As she dances she calls to each one of us in her own way, saying that she is both death and life and that she can teach us, through her movements, the motions of the world itself — with its cycles and seasons, its patterns and rhythms. Streams of energy flow from one hand to another and everything about her being is related to motion. There is no constancy, no sense of being able to stand back and watch. We embrace her in the life-force, and dance with her.

Now a circle of misty light comes up around us and we feel we are dancing in the dawn of the first days of the world. And yet we know that our journey has just begun. We have made our first venture into the underworld of myth and legend, and we must continue.

We call now for an ally, one who can help us attain new heights of mystical vision. A deep blue haze has formed around us but within it, having answered our call, is Sagittarius the centaur. He is a magnificent figure, with the robust muscles of a warrior and the bodily form of a stallion. He is bearded and has friendly eyes that twinkle as we behold him. Meanwhile we notice above him a magnificent rainbow that has manifested in the heavens.

In his right hand Sagittarius holds a magnificent golden bow and as we contemplate it he explains that it has magical qualities. For he can fire arrows into the sky which shower golden light, and which open for us a pathway to a higher place in the cosmic sky.

We watch a golden flare . . . a magnificent array of sparkling lights which marks a new pathway for us. We are drawn by its power, drawn by its magnetism, and we are rising in the air, rising, floating, floating, floating . . .

As we float in the sky we are overwhelmed by the beauty of the luminescent particles of the arrow flare and these droplets now flow together in a path which has become a river. We

39

gather momentum in the current which seems to be drawing us towards the sun. We experience an exalted sense of freedom, of liberation, as we float in the ocean of the sky . . .

Now, as we contemplate the nature of the tide that is carrying us along, we see that it has brought us into a strange domain. Looking to either side, we see as we look closely that one side of the stream has become dark while the other retains the luminosity of the new day and the two aspects seem to mingle in the stream of light that bears us along. We know now that we are pursuing a path of delicate and profound balance. Still the fibres of energy draw us along and we become increasingly one with the stream.

Now we see that this sacred domain also has a guardian and he has an imposing form. We are given his name: *Raphael* . . . He is an enormous winged figure with trailing orange and blue drapes and he stands majestically before us. In his right hand he holds a water vessel and in his left a glowing torch.

At first we cannot clearly see his face, for it is sheathed in light. But our attention is drawn to his chest and the decorative embroidery upon his cloak. We see here, in essence, the fabric of the whole universe . . . a bright vibrant sun shines from his breastplate and circling around it we observe the motion of all the planets and constellations. Raphael says to us: 'You see that the sun and his companion stars in the dark night of the heavens are brothers and sisters'.

Then the golden luminosity in his chest fuses with the glow around his head and his whole form is ablaze with light. Gradually we are able to adjust our vision and we see that he has one foot in the stream and one upon dry land. And he is the overlord of two creatures as well.

One of these is a ruddy lion which lies angrily scowling near his foot. The other is a silver eagle on his left, whose wings whip ferociously in the air in an act of defiance. But we do not fear them because we are in the presence of the Lord Guardian.

He tells us now that he will show us how to control their tenacious qualities. Uplifting his water vessel from the stream, he pours its silvery glistening waters upon the head of the lion. The crystal fluids seem to pour right through him, and he is

40

instantly transformed and subservient to his master. Then the Lord Guardian lowers his torch above the head of the eagle, which seems then to be of glass, reflecting the glowing embers of the torch. A spark of flame falls down into the eagle's heart and fills its entire translucent body with an orange-red glow. And the eagle ceases any longer to menace his master.

Again the Lord Guardian addresses us, reminding us that we are transforming our very being. His voice speaks to us in its own special way and, as we listen, it becomes like music, a mantra, a visionary rhythm which has special significance for each of us. We listen, listen, listen . . .

He beckons us now to enter his domain and we follow the stream of life towards a mountain cleft between two commanding peaks. We see pinky golden rays of the rising sun lighting the mountain. We see the sun eroding the shadows on the mountain slopes, and it is rising slowly, slowly, higher and higher, and we are riding in the stream, feeling the healing rays of light get warmer and warmer upon us. We are merging with its beauty. We feel a deep, deep peace, a deep, deep peace, and we rejoice in its sacred, cleansing light . . .

Guided magical visualisations, or pathworkings, like the one described above, are not in themselves a new approach. However most magical groups have neglected these 'occult mind games' in favour of ceremonial and ritual activities. Dion Fortune, a member of the Stella Matutina which derived from the Order of the Golden Dawn, developed the pathworking technique to tap archetypal images and 'ancient cult memories' which she believed may have derived from previous incarnations. Guided imagery work has since become an important part of the activities of the occult order known as the Servants of the Light, based in St Helier on the island of Jersey. Founded by Dion Fortune's disciple W.E. Butler, the SOL, under present director Dolores Ashcroft-Nowicki, encourages its occult members to develop the powers of visualisation necessary for pathworkings.

In 1979 i had the good fortune to meet three practising members of SOL who had been experimenting with new pathworking techniques. We found that we had a great deal in common and soon began undertaking 'magical journeys' together. Cheryl, Moses and Cathy had begun to break down the linear structure of guided pathworkings and were writing new 'entry' material themselves that focused on specific magical symbols or mystical deities without constricting or enclosing the journey. The visualisation led only to a certain point, but no further. After that you were on your own! This modification of technique allowed for a great deal more spontaneity and, in a sense, was more challenging. Now, instead of being summoned under tight controls, the gods were being invited to speak on their own terms!

The technique itself was completely simple. One person would read the entry visualisation aloud while the others relaxed and flowed meditatively with the imagery. After each journey was completed — a process often taking around quarter of an hour — the contents of the visionary sequence were immediately written down. We would wait until everyone was 'back' and had recorded an account of the journey before discussing what had happened.

One day Moses proposed a meeting with Merlin and the Jaguar. I didn't even know that Merlin *had* a jaguar but I was willing to chance it! Perhaps Moses was deliberately throwing aside orthodox mythology to allow the imagination more free rein? As we gathered in Cathy's small inner-city flat I wondered what was in store. Moses has a deep and haunting voice and the charm of a great storyteller. As we lay on the floor, completely relaxed and breathing slow, deep breaths, he began to read to us:

> Imagine a wall in front of you, with a doorway. You stand in front of the doorway and try to see what is on the other side. All you can see is a black mist filling the doorway. You step through the mist and find yourself on the edge of a clearing. In the centre of the clearing is a statue of a jaguar made of green jade. Of this stone tiger, this beast 'made of living water turned to stone,' it is said that if you sit on its back it may come to life

42

and take you wherever it may take you . . .

Beside the statue of the jaguar stands a man, an old man
with long white hair and beard. He wears a long, white robe.
He is Merlin, the Lord of the Jaguar.

Step into the clearing and begin your journey . . .

My experience was quite intense and much more dramatic
than I expected:

It is easy visualising Merlin although he seems also like an
ancient Greek sage — the archetypal wise man. The statue of
the jaguar is considerably larger than Merlin, and the giant cat
is poised as if ready to strike. Looking up towards the heavens,
it sits upright on its rear legs . . .

As I draw near, I allow the jaguar to jump and devour me, as
it strikes for my heart. I am surprised that I do not die but
instead find that I have conquered the jaguar, who has now
become my ally. He is immediately more subdued, and I am
able to ride on his back.

We soar into the heavens and it is very dark. At times I seem
to see another jaguar alongside us, but it is really Leo the Lion
striding through the constellations in the night sky.

I feel some degree of dissociation as the darkness intensifies.
The jaguar is taking me down, not upwards as I wished! It is
another trial of strength. It is now time for me to become
Merlin myself. The change takes place . . . I feel I *am* Merlin. I
am in control and the trial is over. Still in a state of slight
dissociation, I awaken and gradually recover full consciousness
of my surroundings.

This journey gave me two valuable insights. The first was that
I should never underestimate the power of the internal
mythic images as they became increasingly real within the
field of consciousness. The second was not to panic at
moments of overwhelming crisis. On many occasions since
this journey I have been devoured by my magical ally, but
death seems to be no barrier at all in the imagination — the
magician invariably finds that he can keep bouncing back! I
have learnt also that no image should ever be allowed to
dominate the consciousness so strongly as to cause a retreat;

this indicates a lack of control. Far better to go with the flow of images, even if they seem to contradict logic completely . . . And of course, in magical reality there is no logic at all. Everything is possible. One soon learns to take a stand with both feet planted firmly in the clouds:

Cathy also had an interesting and evocative journey with the jaguar:

> The jaguar comes alive and Merlin and I mount on its back. Merlin seems to merge with the body of the jaguar but still retains his shape also. We leap into the sky in one enormous bound, over the top of the trees ringing the glade. We fly over mountains and valleys, trees and plains. Higher and higher we fly until we are above the clouds, flying on into the sunset itself — and to the land behind the sun.
>
> We finally come down through the clouds and land in a green field where some people are sitting in a circle. There are fires blazing and a bard is playing a harp. Merlin dismounts with me and the jaguar is frozen back into immobility. Merlin turns to me and says 'These are my people'. As we walk among them they make a kind of obeisance to him, by touching their hands to their faces.
>
> We sit in the main circle and a bard sings a song of a drowned city. This city, or town, was by the coast and people made a rich living from the sea and the surrounding land, which was very fertile. In the beginning they gave thanks to their Gods, bringing gifts in appreciation. But as time passed they forgot from whom their wealth came, and they grew greedier. Finally they became so corrupt that the Gods rose in anger and caused the water to rise, drowning their city and submerging all the land around them . . .
>
> The whole scene and story seems incredibly familiar to me, and I feel a real kinship with these people, and a great sense of belonging. When the bard has finished his song I ask Merlin if I may speak with him, and Merlin agrees. I feel very close to the bard, who is young and golden, but his eyes contain at the same time an expression of great age and sadness. He hands me his harp and I play it. I sing the song of my own journey —

my searching and yearning — and the people listen, finally it is time to go. But I feel as though at last I have come home, and have found the place of my own roots, my beginning.

We mount the jaguar and Merlin holds me as we fly. He tells me I am one of his people. As we land he kisses me on my forehead, and this activates a silver star of energy. I am bathed in an intense white light and Merlin tells me to return whenever I wish.

It was obvious that the new, less structured pathworkings were capable of unleashing a very rich source of imagery.

Cathy's tale, quite aside from the parallel with the Atlantis legend, had shown her her own psychic origins. She had found her place in the mythic cosmos and, in a very profound and personal way, had discovered magical allies previously unknown to her. All of us were deeply moved as Cathy related her story, and I was intrigued by the potential of these less formal magical pathworkings.

On another occasion we undertook a journey somewhat comparable to the mind games except that we ascended rather than descended into the unconscious. And rather than be guided all the way, this time the entry visualisation offered us a three-fold choice. Cheryl read her entry to us:

> You are standing at the foot of a spiral staircase of very simple design. You commence the climb. Up and around it leads you, until at last you emerge in the centre of a very strange chamber. It is triangular, and in each of its three walls is set a white door. Approaching one of the doors you see an inscription which says:
>
> 'There is sweet music here'
>
> . . . and moving further around you read the inscription on the next door:
>
> 'There is a play within'
>
> . . . and the last door says:
>
> 'Buried treasure'
>
> Return now to the centre of the hall and choose which door, if any, you wish to pass through. Enter that door to find what is waiting, knowing that you may return whenever you wish.

On this occasion I chose the doorway leading to buried treasure, I suppose because it sounded the most spectacular. However it soon became apparent to me that the treasure was not personal wealth but a metaphor for self-realisation and gifts of a visionary kind:

> I am assailed by a group of motley, bizarre creatures who hurl missiles at me and who roll their bodies into wheels, obstructing my pathway. I persevere, and come to the domain of a winged griffin who sits in a cave filled with golden light. His body glistens with radiance and at first it seems that a treasure hoard lies all around this awesome creature. The griffin tells me that the treasure itself is of a paradoxical nature. If I overcome the griffin and gather the treasure into my possession, claiming it as my own, I am bound to lose it. The treasure is only meaningful, he tells me, if I fail to be dazzled by it, and if I recognise that it has always belonged to me — in fact, to everybody. The griffin says he serves as a

reminder to people approaching the hoard of treasure as a goal, that the journey itself is an illusion. I am impressed by this advice and wake up empty-handed. I have not attempted to assail the griffin for his treasure.

Needless to say, I found this Zen-like journey extremely meaningful. In the west, our cultural upbringing attunes us to strive for goals and to acquire wealth in order to improve the quality of our lives. Sometimes we forget what we possess already!

Now it was my turn to prepare entry visualisations for the group. The first of these was an entry to The Empress, the archetypal Great Mother of the Universe, and a central figure from the Major Arcana of the Tarot. This time, as I read the visualisation to the others I found I was also able to continue with the journey myself, something I hadn't thought possible:

We enter a cave door and descend by a flight of ancient stone steps to the palace of the Empress. At the bottom of the steps we come to a magnificent door encrusted with silver discs and beautiful sea-blue gemstones. The door swings in and we enter the ante-chamber. The floor is pearly and translucent and the walls of the chamber shimmer like starlit mirrors.

A young maiden presents herself as mistress of the star-chamber and we tell her that we would like to meet the Empress. The maiden says that she may allow us to enter one of three doorways and that she will give us a gift to enable us to be effective in the Goddess's domain.

The gifts are: — a scythe with which to harvest wheat
                 — a silver goblet from which to drink
                 — a luminous crystal to guide us beneath a lake

We see symbols of these on the doorways before us and take our gifts to enter. We are told that when we meet the Goddess we should account for ourselves, telling her in what manner we have travelled in her domain and what we have learnt. And now we step forward . . .

The imagery took effect immediately:

> In the ante-chamber the gift that I nominated from the maiden was the goblet from which to drink. Almost immediately I was aware that I was in a different domain. I was travelling on a precipitous mountain track which climbed perilously above me on a very vertical incline. I had a guide — a youth with a beautifully proportioned body and superb golden hair, and who carried a fiery torch. The glow lit the landscape and it was craggy with green/blue colouring and potentially very hard to climb. I seemed to follow the light rather than watch where my feet were.
>
> Then I was aware of a coiled dragon above me, curved around the central peak of the mountain. A warrior came forward and slew the dragon and then his own head was cut off. I didn't see how this occurred but a sense of self-sacrifice was implied. I passed by, and came towards the great Empress seated on her throne. She had long, flowing golden hair but I found it difficult to focus on her face as if her eyes were in many places at once.
>
> She held out another flask for me to drink — instead, I was not aware of actually having taken the goblet from the maiden in the first place and maybe the sacred drink was the goal, not a gift given initially. I drank, and as the fluid poured into me I felt I was expanding and could almost float away. It was a very liberating, expansive feeling and it seemed that something precious had been given to me.

I found this a very satisfying journey and it was the beginning of a number of encounters with sacred beings where some sort of gift would be bestowed. Usually, I found out, the actual properties of the gift would be intangible, even if the object was familiar. The giving of a gift seemed to symbolise a degree of interaction in itself much more significant than the gift itself. Later, in the shamanic work, I would discover that many of the gifts were power objects, energy sources planted directly within my body by the sacred beings themselves.

On Cheryl's journey to the Empress, she was asked to give a gift to the Goddess, not the other way around! Her journey began by combining two of her magical options, rather than focusing on just one:

Through the doorway is a field of wheat which I work, with others, to harvest. When it is complete we return to their village for a celebration, during which a youth tells me I might reach the Empress through the caves in the Misty Mountains.

I journey towards the moutains and on my way I am approached by an old man with a dog at his heels. He offers his services as a guide but I refuse. He then gives me a gift saying 'This is your pearl', and leaves me.

The caves are made of limestone, full of strange and beautiful formations. The luminous crystal I have been given as a gift by the maiden of the ante-chamber lights the caves beautifully. Rivulets run everywhere but I have no real difficulty in passing through. I leave the crystal to shine in the caves.

Finally I pass through a door to the Empress. Her hair is of gold and silver, elaborately arranged in the form of a rising sun. She asks for a gift and I reply that I have not brought one. She says she would like the pearl. I am loath to part with it, but I give it to her and she places it on the floor. Softly touching it, she makes it grow until it becomes a huge, translucent dome.

A doorway appears and I step inside. The pearl chamber is silent and peaceful and yet I tingle with a kind of vibration. In the centre is a column of water which, because the liquid is not flowing, seems to be suspended in time. I stand in this column as if to blend with it, and here the voyage ends.

The next journey I prepared was a brave one indeed — to the domain of Abraxas. I was very pleased with the entry material after I had written it, both from the viewpoint of the symbolism, and also because in the form of the waterfall I had found a dynamic visual image for propelling the meditator into a new dimension:

We look into the sky and are overwhelmed by the radiant beauty of the sun which radiates light that falls to earth in the form of fiery droplets. The droplets begin to shower in a golden haze. Days pass, then months, and by the time a year has passed the luminescent shower has become a wide river.

We journey down the river in a strange, archaic vessel that seems oriental — perhaps Persian or Indian — and which is painted so that one side is black and the other white. We gather momentum on the golden stream and are suddenly aware that we are approaching a waterfall and that the boat is quite incapable of avoiding floating over the edge. We do so, and the feeling is one of liberation and freedom.

We float in the ocean of the sky and are once again aware of a golden haze. As we draw nearer to the source of this light we perceive a strange and awesome deity whose name we are told is Abraxas.

Abraxas has a human body, the head of a hawk and legs of serpents. In his left hand he holds a dagger and in the right an ancient shield. Abraxas says that he can offer to lead us into the land of night or the land of day and that whatever our choice he will protect us with his weapons. He takes us to his temple, a superb and majestic structure which stands on the peak of a high mountain. There are two gateways in the temple from which we may choose to commence our journey of the magical spheres. One will lead us to the nightland and the other to the kingdom of the new day, but we will not know until we enter . . . for indeed Abraxas is an unpredictable and awesome god.

However, we must be courageous in his presence for he is protecting us. We make our choice of doorway and enter . . .

Once again I found I was able to participate in the visionary process released by the visualisation:

I enter the right door of the temple of Abraxas. It has high arches inside and a seemingly infinite heavenly vault. There are people here, holding their hands heavenwards, and I am aware of a fluttering motion. At first I think it is a palpitating heart, then a sacrifice, but now I see a white dove flying aloft. I feel extremely peaceful and inwardly reassured.

Now I dwell on the form of Abraxas. He is very much a composite, his hawk-like head suggesting he is a god of flight and ecstasy while his body belongs to man's domain. His serpent legs reach down below the earth. Now Abraxas

50

changes form and I am shown a night-owl with angry yellow eyes in the place of Abraxas's hawk head. He pecks at my heart, but I allow him to — for I know that I cannot be harmed. Abraxas is showing me his night-side, but I do not feel any sense of panic. I am given to understand that these are the two facets of a great high-god who lives in the clouds in the ceiling of the celestial chamber. I am told that Abraxas holds the key for passing beyond this domain, but I remain within it and feel a protective sense of peace.

I was very nervous before this pathworking. I knew from Jung's account, and also from the Gnostic literature that Abraxas was difficult to fathom and certainly impossible to predict! On many inner-plane occasions since, I have been attacked and even devoured by magical creatures but have always found it best to yield rather than panic. It would of course be quite normal to fear actual death and to sense the imminent destruction of the ego, but inevitably one comes through these experiences with a feeling of renewal or integration.

Moses' encounter with Abraxas proved to be much more testing than mine, and he engaged himself in a struggle with the god, although it was not without its humorous moments. Unlike the experiences of Cathy, Cheryl and myself, Moses' often had a strong conversational content:

I enter through the right door. There are stepping-stones which are like pillar tops in the water. The pillars become taller and taller, reaching into deep space. The last one I have to leap across. Abraxas speaks: 'Now you must fight me'.

He suddenly has wings and swoops into the air and down towards me. I grab his snake legs and he zooms up into the air with me. It is as if he has bird claws clutching my scalp, as I clutch his feet. It is like being on a circus trapeze. Then far below I notice a silver dome on the ground. He brings me down. 'Call me when you want to go back'. He swoops up into the air again. I sit on the silver dome and then a giant white worm comes and circles around me. Abraxas comes zooming down. I catch his snake legs and he rises up with me. Again, it

51

is like being at a circus. I am twirling round and round, holding onto his right serpent-leg.

'Now let go — if you dare'

(I let go and I can fly. It is beautiful, slow-motion sequence)

'Now you must fight me'

(I have a sword in my right hand and a shield to the left. Abraxas changes his knife into his right hand and his shield to the left to oblige me. We perform a mock battle — clashing weapons and shields as we fly into space. Now I drop my shield and I am falling down, down, down . . . but there is a net stretching across space which propels me back again . . .)

'It is time to go back'

(I grab the snake legs and we come shooting out through the temple doorway and land)

'Abraxas?', I ask, 'What was the meaning of what I saw and did?'

'The images are mine, the meanings must be yours', he tells me.

'What was the experience?'

'A testing'

'A testing of whom?'

'Of you, and also of me'

'Who was the tested and who the testing one?'

'You were the tester. I was the tested one. The snake did not bite you . . . ' (a reference to my holding his snake legs?)

'What was the silver dome?'

'A tortoise'

'What was the worm?'

'I know not'

'What was the net?'

'The rising of the sun'

Abraxas continues: 'Go back my child, with my blessing. Go back my child with fear. Go back my child with loving.'

We were finding the pathworkings extremely interesting and evocative. Each evening as we gathered for a new journey we had the sense of a magical adventure before us. We were enjoying the ventures into the symbolic, mythic areas of our imagination because they were exciting and full of personal meaning — although we were not always able to pin down analytically just what that meaning was. One of the feelings which we all experienced at various times was the sense of participating in a personal fairy-tale, of being able to transform from one shape or location to another, all in the blink of an eyelid!

I did not realise at the time that the pathworkings were leading me towards shamanism. I possibly should have been aware of this direction because the journeys were really a form of light trance produced by a combination of will-power, visualisation and relaxation, and the shamanic journey of the spirit — familiar to me from anthropological reports — had many features in common. The first shamanic content finally presented itself during a pathworking based on the symbol of the Tao, in which my journey was seemingly quite unrelated to the entry symbol. Once again, Moses read to us with his warm expressive voice:

> Imagine yourself in a dim temple of oriental design. In the centre of the temple sits an ancient monk whose eyes are sightless, and yet he smiles. Across the blind monk's knees lies a long-handled object, and behind him is a huge gong. Depicted on the gong are two fish, one of black, the other of white. And you recognise the disc of Tao, which is the gong. And you realise that the object across the old man's knees may be used to strike the gong. If you choose to remain and act, it may be that you will hear the striking of the gong of Tao, and learn something of its voice. Do then, as you will . . .

My journey was a curious one:

> I do not strike the gong but notice instead that the *yin yang* circle of the fishes becomes a doorway to a tunnel which leads down through waves to a place in the underworld. I am told that I am journeying to the domain of the sea-goddess Sedna (an Eskimo deity familiar to me from anthropological accounts of shamanic practices) and that my task will be a difficult one.
> Sedna seems to be guarded by fierce tigers (I certainly

wasn't expecting those!) and I can see their teeth snarling with rage. Later I notice that the waves of the stormy sea raging around Sedna's domain are not waves at all, but wolves who protect her from the unwary. And yet I am still confident that I will snatch a glimpse of her.

As it turns out, it is only a momentary flash, but I see her twice. On the first occasion I see her in the distance, standing in front of her throne. She has wild hair which lashes back from her forehead and a robe falls loosely around her form, exposing one of her breasts. Her manner is very hostile but after I have been able to prove that I am immune to the sea-wolves a new sense of calm comes over me. A serene wash of blue sweeps into my vision. I summon the water pentagram to view and vibrate the water mantra 'Shaddai' (techniques learnt from western magic) but the goddess does not come. I call her by her name, Sedna the Sea Goddess, and I seem to float into an underwater cave. I have flashes of old men asleep, but then find myself at the foot of her throne. I look up and she towers above me. Whether I sit at the base of a huge column or whether her form is huge I cannot tell, but I desperately want to see her face. This is not granted to me.

I ask her to pour her waters into my body and I feel that to a degree, but not totally, this request is granted. She tells me that I should come to see her again. Then I catch a glimpse of her face, mirrored in the waves, but like a glassy haze it disappears. I know I will have to go back to see her.

It was surprising enough finding myself on a symbolic pathway to Sedna's domain, and the imagery of the sea of wolves was extraordinary, but the next journey gave me my first inkling of my magical allies. Moses had been interested in psycho-drama and symbolic role-play for some time, and one night — on his suggestion — we decided to try something different.

Moses had cleared the main room in the small, semi-detached house so that it was almost totally devoid of furniture. The room was perfectly square except for the area built up around what had been an open fireplace, and which now constituted a fifth wall across one of the corners. It was here that we decided the ritual shaman would sit on a small chair, presiding over the sacred space and either drumming or shaking the gourd rattles we had brought for the purpose. Moses proposed that he would take the shaman role while I would summon an animal spirit and begin to dance its characteristics in spontaneous ritual form, within the cleared space. Moses suggested that as the impressions began to come through strongly I should retire to the corridor and prepare a mask from paper, wool and crayons that had been put aside. Moses, as presiding shaman, would then summon me to come forth from the corridor and return to the main room, wearing the mask and dancing in league with the magical ally as the drum-beat intensified.

The room was now darkened and illuminated by a solitary candle. Moses took his position on the chair and after a while began to beat a mantric rhythm on the large flat drum. I called forth several times seeking an animal spirit and then began to loosen my body in spontaneous dance gestures as Moses increased the beat of the drum. The image of a large hawk flashed into vision several times. I went out to the corridor, made myself a rudimentary hawk's-head mask with paper and crayons, donned it and began to dance hesitantly into the main room. The effect was eerie. I had made eye-holes in the mask but my vision was extremely constricted. In the darkness I could make out the figure of Moses seated in the distance. He looked stern and remote, his dark curly black hair and beard lost in the shadows flickering around the candle.

I began to dance the hawk in front of him, my arms moving freely in an undulating fashion suggestive of flight. The energies of the hawk now seemed to rise up within me and, beckoning to my shaman guide, I asked him to dance with me. Our wings rose and fell in slow, rhythmic fashion as we whirled around the room and I began to lose all awareness of the space we were occupying. Instead, I found we were soaring to the peak of a sacred mountain. It was an exhilarating flight. The earth was now far below us, lost in the distance, as I became — for a timeless moment — the large and awesome hawk that had presented itself as my magical ally. Exhausted from the dance, I sank down on the floor and returned to the more familiar location of the small room in the house in Trafalgar Street. For a while I was unsure what had occurred. My body had felt alive with a new energy yet now I was physically tired and strained by the experience. I wondered what sort of magical reality Moses and I had tapped into, and where my hawk image had come from.

As it turned out, it was not long before I was provided with some of the answers.

CHAPTER FIVE

The Shaman's Doorway

Moses and I had heard that the International Transpersonal Association was holding its 1980 annual conference in Australia. Several leading members of the Human Potential Movement associated with the Esalen Institute, including Stanislav Grof, James Fadiman, and Ralph Metzner, were to give papers. We made enquiries through the Australian organisers at the Blackwood Centre in Victoria, and to our surprise and delight both Moses and I were asked to give papers and workshops as part of the conference proceedings. Moses was to deliver a workshop based on 'Death and the Soul', including story-telling, mythodrama and the ritual use of masks and fantasy. I agreed to present the Major Arcana of the Tarot as an initiatory sequence using the superb slides prepared by the Servants of the Light. I also suggested a guided imagery session which would take participants up the Middle Pillar of the Tree of Life to the accompaniment of appropriate electronic music. Unfortunately Moses became sick prior to the conference and could not attend, but I was able to present the core of the material that I had found to be most valuable in tapping the essence of the magical tradition. These sessions went well. However the conference had a strange aftermath for me as a result of an unexpected contact.

Anthropologist Michael Harner was attending the conference to give lectures and workshops on the shamanic journey. Harner was well known to me through his excellent

The shaman's magical universe. An illustration by Martin Carey
Courtesy: The Woodstock Aquarian

scholarly works on shamanism and had been the reader for my Masters thesis. He had been a visiting professor at Columbia, Yale and Berkeley and, understandably, I had an image of him as a solid and thoroughly respectable academic. I hardly expected him to be a shaman as well! Harner had arrived at the conference carrying a shaman's drum, gourd rattles, and a set of feathers and bones used by the Salish Indians for a mind-control game. As a result of his extensive field research in the Upper Amazon, Mexico and western North America, he had learnt shamanic techniques from the Indians and was now adapting their approach for a western audience, showing how we too could tap the inner magical universe.

Harner's lectures and workshops were superb. Harner was a large friendly man with a dense black beard and mischievous dark eyes, who would chuckle when presenting the paradoxes of the shaman's universe. He told us about power animals and magical forces in Nature without at all attempting to present a logical rationale. He explained how, for the Jivaro Indians, a man can only reach maturity if protected by special power allies that accompany that person and provide vitality and purpose. He showed us how to meditate on the mantric, repetitive rhythm of a beating drum and ride it into the inner world, journeying in the mind's eye down the root system of the cosmic tree or up smoke tunnels into the sky. He asked us not to judge these events when they occurred to us but to dwell with them on their own terms. We were, he said, entering a shamanic mode of trance consciousness where *anything* could happen — and invariably did! But because we saw strange, surreal events, or mythic animals in unfamiliar locales, we should not recoil from that but participate in the process of discovering a new visionary universe within ourselves.

Harner's workshop technique was remarkably simple. After blessing the group with his rattles, Harner would start pounding his large flat drum and encourage us to dance free-form around the room with our eyes half-closed, attuning

59

ourselves to any expression that would flow through. We were endeavouring to contact our magical allies in a manner rather similar to the way Moses and I had stumbled on by ourselves.

After quite a short while, many people adopted animal postures and forms, and began to express these spontaneously in very individual ways. Some people became bears and lumbered slowly around the room. Others became snakes or lizards. There were several wild cats, the occasional elephant and a variety of birds. Once again my eagle-hawk presented itself to me as I winged around through the group.

Harner then asked us to lie down on the floor and close our eyes. He would begin drumming in a monotonous rhythm, to allow us to ride down into the shamanic underworld. Harner had explained to us that this was not an 'evil' domain but simply the magical 'reverse' of our familiar, day-to-day world, a place where a different kind of reality prevailed. The technique was to imagine yourself entering the trunk of a large tree through a door at its base. Perhaps there were steps inside but soon one would see the roots leading down at an angle of around 45°. Following a root-tunnel you then wound down, down, down — all the time propelled and supported by the constancy of the drumming. Finally you would see a speck of light at the end of the tunnel. Gradually drawing towards it you had to pass through into the light and look around at the new surroundings. Various animals would pass by, but we were asked to look for one that presented itself to us four times. That animal was possibly our own magical ally. Perhaps we would engage in conversation, be shown new vistas and landscapes in Nature, fly in the air, or be given gifts or special knowledge. Harner emphasised that any of these things could happen but it was up to us to accept the visionary experience on its own level. If elephants finished up flying through the air, so be it. There was no question of the experience being put down as 'just imagination'. Imagination, in Harner's view, was a different type of reality, not an illusory world to be rationalised or belittled.

60

Since my first guided imagery journeys I have always kept records of my experiences, and invariably I have written them down immediately afterwards so that all the details remained in a clear sequence. The following is my record of the first shamanic journey at the Transpersonal Conference:

> I summon the image of the huge angophora tree that grows in the garden next door to ours at home, and pass through a doorway at its base. Using the rhythm of Michael's drumming I ride along the root system of the tree, down into the earth. The tunnel is large enough to flow down with ease, and I go through various twists and bends as I follow the root system.
>
> We have been taught to flow towards the light, and yet it seems to be a considerable length of time before the flickering light of day trickles in through the end of the tunnel.
>
> I find myself in a lush, primeval glade with huge, soaring trees reaching for the sky amid trailing vines and creepers. The undergrowth is quite dense and the trunks of the trees rise majestically to an enormous height. I am immediately aware, through an array of images, that my power animal is a hawk — confirming the earlier experiment with Moses in Sydney. I look for the home of the hawk and am immediately transported to a nest at the top of the tree. I see the hawk very clearly and seem to merge with it for a while. Its wingspan is impressive and I hear its cry.
>
> I am pleased that this creature seems to be my ally in the underworld. Coming back, I re-enter the tunnel and rise to the surface . . .

Encouraged by both the directness and essential simplicity of the shamanic technique, I decided to participate in a day-long workshop that Michael Harner was holding in Melbourne after the conference. We were asked to minimise our food intake and I managed to restrict my diet to an apple and a small piece of cheese for the whole day — a considerable effort!

As we gathered in the large hall, Harner took us through the same techniques that he had explained earlier. In addition we also paired off within the group so we could practise contacting power animals on behalf of others — bringing the magical allies up the tunnel in order to transfer them to our partners. The theory behind this was the Indian concept that disease was linked to soul-loss. One of us would pretend to be 'dis-spirited' while the other would take the role of shaman and seek a power animal as a source of new vitality for that person. After an animal offered itself in the shamanic world we would scurry mentally back up the tunnel with the animal held close in our arms. We would then 'breathe' it into the chest and head of our partner, imagining that at that time its essence was transferring to the sick person.

We also did a great deal of dancing, and soon our power allies began to present themselves much more spontaneously in our movements and gestures. I am sure that much of this activity provided an appropriate environment and atmosphere for our magical journeys. We seemed to be entering a quite new dimension which soon became as familiar and real as the outside world. My first journey took me through both night and day, and my link with the hawk was now much more specific:

I travel down the tunnel beneath the angophora and this time take less time to reach the light at the end of the tunnel. However, there is a problem: the tunnel has opened onto a cliff-face with a precipitous drop to the sea. I have to summon my power animal to *me* . . . The hawk appears in the distance, flying with its wings gracefully extended. It has powerful dark black and yellow eyes and a mix of black and brown feathers. As it approaches the cave entrance it turns around, allowing me to mount up on its back. We ease away, flying over the sea.

It is daylight at this stage. We come along the cliff-edge and I see a domed building overlooking the sea. Then there is a very clear scene of a building like a restaurant — with white stucco walls — fronting onto the sea. A large number of tourists are clustering around.

Leaving them, we now fly into the sky and night falls. I seem to merge once again with the hawk as we fly over a hamlet with a number of high-gabled houses huddled together. The darkness shrouds them but their ancient medieval roofs peer through.

Now it is daytime again and I land amidst a crowd at a fairground. The people seem pleased to see the hawk land, and they welcome us. Then we rise up again, and darkness returns. We fly over the sea, moonlight glinting over the waves. Rocky crags reach up out of the sea, but I feel secure. I can see the original rock face in the distance. I enter, and return up the root system to the tree in my garden.

The feeling of entering into a new experiential domain was very impressive. It really did seem at the time that I was flying, and I could see the waves of the sea crashing against the rocks beneath me. These journeys seem distinctly different from dreams; the imagery is much clearer and at times seems like watching a film — except that one is actually participating in it!

The climax to the the workshop, for me, came in the evening. Harner told us that he had been experimenting with journeys up into the sky, as well as down into the underworld. He asked us to imagine entering a smoke tunnel either by wafting upwards on smoke from a campfire or by entering a fireplace and soaring towards the sky up a chimney. As we entered the smoke tunnel, he explained, we would see it unfolding before us, taking us higher and higher into the sky. At some time or other, Harner said, a water bird would present itself as an ally, to lift us still higher into the sky-world. Why this should be a water bird was not explained. He was also keen to see whether any of us would see any 'geometric structures', although he didn't wish to elaborate on this in case his comments had the effect of programming us into a specific visionary experience. As it turned out, several people in the group had visions of geometric, 'celestial' architecture.

The room was quite dark as Harner began to beat on his drum. I found it easy to visualise the fireplace in our front room:

I enter the fireplace and quickly shoot up the chimney into a lightish grey whirling cloud tunnel. Soon I am aware of my guardian — a pelican with a pink beak.

Mounting the pelican's back I ride higher with it into the smoke tunnel. In the distance I see a golden mountain rising in the mist . . .

As we draw closer I see that, built on the top of the mountain, is a magnificent palace made of golden crystal, radiating lime-yellow light. I am told that this is the palace of the phoenix, and I then see that golden bird surmounting the edifice. It seems to be connected with my own power-hawk.

I feel awed and amazed by the beauty of this place, but the regal bird bids me welcome. Then the hawk comes forward and places a piece of golden crystal in my chest. I hold my breath deeply as I receive it, for it is a special gift.

The drum is still sounding but soon Michael asks us to return. However I am still high in the sky and find it very difficult to re-enter the smoke tunnel. When I finally do begin to return the heavens remain golden, and as I travel down into the tunnel I look up to see saint-like figures rimming the tunnel, farewelling me . . .

This journey was a very awesome one for me. After returning to an awareness of the workshop location and the people around me, I found it very difficult to articulate my thoughts. I seemed lost for words but anxious, nevertheless, to communicate some of the importance that the journey had had for me. I felt I had been in a very sacred space. The direct interaction with the hawk that had planted a crystal in my chest was totally unexpected, although I remembered reading about events like that in Aboriginal mythology.

There was a minor embarrassment as well. Some of the people attending Harner's workshop had also been to the Transpersonal Conference and had participated in my guided imagery session using Tarot imagery and electronic music. Many of them had told me afterwards that they had got a lot out of it. Now, by contrast, I found myself in a state of mind where I had experienced a quite different type of magical reality that seemed to go beyond anything I had achieved in western magic. There was a total directness and natural authenticity in the shamanic journey. Harner's notion that shamanism pre-dated the split of Eastern and Western religious consciousness also gave it a primeval quality which added to its appeal. Suddenly shamanism seemed much more valid and real, and in our group discussion — when I finally did manage to assemble some thoughts — I made this point to the other people present. Events since then have shown me that this idea of a split between magic and shamanism is quite illusory and one can tap a universal mythology through both methods. In fact, as I was to discover, at times the two traditions fuse together. Nevertheless, at the time, I was convinced that I had found something else. I returned to Sydney delighted with having made so many good contacts at the Transpersonal Conference, a definite convert to shamanism.

CHAPTER SIX

Hawk and Crocodile

Several of my close friends were interested in visionary magic. Cheryl had found our magical pathworkings extremely evocative and she wanted to try the shamanic technique. A friend from the conference, Sue, and Ly — who had spent many years with Nature worship, Wicca and western magic — were also keen to explore the new approach. Through 1981 we held regular shaman gatherings at each other's homes. One of us would drum while the others would journey on the vision quest. The following are entries from my magical records of that period:

January 28

I find it easy enough to get into the tunnel and rise upwards. I am soon aware of a bird coming to get me. It is delicate, yet broad in wingspan, and has a long curved beak. I think it is a heron but am told it is a curlew.

We fly upwards and come again to the domain of golden crystal although it is not as well defined as before. But my power bird — magnificent ally! — is there, and faces me directly. This time instead of receiving a gift from him, I have to reach for it. My hand passes into his neck and from it I take a green gem; bottle-green rather than emerald in hue.

Now the bird shows me his transformations. He passes through a number of forms, the most notable being a pigeon. Perhaps he is telling me that he can be docile and peaceful as well as hostile.

March 2

I travel with the drumbeat through the smoke tunnel and this
time the pelican is there to assist. However the atmosphere is
very turgid and it is difficult to ascend with any speed. It feels
more like a DC–3 than Concorde!

As I rise in the air my first impression is of a huge giant
digging the soil with a spade. He hurls his implement in the air
and I follow it: it has become a totem-pole surmounted with
the image of my hawk.

The pole now rises, rocket-like, into the air and becomes a
torch . . . we are reaching more elevated ground.

I have come to a marbled courtyard and look towards a
stylish palace that combines both futuristic and art deco
architecture — as if belonging both to the past and an era yet
to come.

I enter the hall and it is very dark inside. Through the
shadows I see an Ibis-headed god, seated on a throne. It is a
form of Thoth, presumably, but this is not clear to me.

There is an Egyptian bas-relief on the wall behind the god.
Two hands are visible in profile, holding a flask. The hands
now become three-dimensional and, lifting out from the wall,
pour water onto my head which passes down into my body. I
feel I am turning into glass or crystal.

The drumming has ceased but I still feel quite rigid. It is
some time before I am 'back'.

July 13

I visualise a large door at the base of my angophora. The door
is regal and stately, and I prepare to enter. However, almost
immediately I find forces blocking my entry. A procession of
hostile Egyptian forms, including a 'dark' version of Horus,
impedes my path, and a black swan tries to peck me.

I persevere, and enter the tunnel which by now is full of
people. The hustle and bustle is unpleasant and, again, I have
the feeling that something or someone is barring my way. I
continue to to fight my way along — quite an unexpected
experience — and eventually discover that this tunnel is quite
straight, not twisting like a root system, and I can see quite
clearly where I am going.

The people have formed a stream on either side of me and are now travelling in my direction, not against me. Rather than emerge from the tunnel into the light I notice that the left-hand side of the tunnel has become translucent and the line of people begins to curve outwards. Gradually the figures form a circle which encloses what I take to be a sacred area. Within the circle there is a stylised island surrounded by water. A large tree is growing on the island and I begin to climb it, anticipating an encounter with my hawk. But it is not to be . . .

I become increasingly aware that I am in the presence of a crocodile entity. At first I see him from the side and wonder whether he is a new ally. Gradually I become more and more aware of his snout and his interlocking teeth. I see his eyes quite clearly.

Now he turns full on, and begins to eat me. I yield to him and there is no pain. There is a vague, slightly disquietening feeling that some of my limbs have been separated off, but this is apparently no obstacle, for I continue on my way.

Higher up the tree I come at last to the domain of my hawk. But he is not fully visible, and a quite extraordinary sight presents itself. The 'room' I am in has a layer of dense grey cloud near its 'ceiling' and the legs of the hawk are visible protruding through it. But I am not granted a complete vision of my power animal . . .

Perhaps the hawk is punishing me for not coming to see him more often!

Certain themes seemed to be emerging on these journeys. The power hawk was beginning to show itself to me in different forms and the familiar shamanic images of the power-crystal, the water bird allies, the cosmic tree, and even its symbolic representative the totem pole, continued to appear. However, certain other aspects were puzzling. I seemed to have another power animal in the form of a crocodile. There was certainly no obvious rationale for this since I have never lived in a tropical region and crocodiles have only been of passing interest. Nevertheless, the crocodile has since appeared to me on several occasions.

More surprising than any of these aspects, though, was the

emergence of strong Egyptian imagery on the journeys. My expectation had been that shamanism would strike to to the 'earliest' and 'deepest' core of mythic imagery, and that somehow my experiences would now be more primeval. This was not the case at all. Since my earliest ventures in shamanism, Horus, Ra, Isis, Thoth and other images from classical Egyptian mythology have continually arisen during the visionary journeys and of course they dominate the symbolism of the western mystery tradition and the magic of the Golden Dawn.

One particular journey from this period brought home to me what now seems obvious, namely that shamanism does not confine itself to native Indian symbolism but can tap a vast resource of mythic imagery in the subconscious mind.

I was with Cheryl, Moses and Ly in the Trafalgar Street flat where Moses and I had first experimented with shamanic dance and ritual masks. The evening began in the usual way, and on this occasion Moses was drumming. From the start the journey had a very specific direction:

It is the day before full moon . . .

My initial desire is to undertake a journey of ascent, but it seems that tonight I have no choice but to go down! My eagle-hawk is there and immediately offers to carry me down the tunnel on his back.

We come out over fierce, lashing waves and the scenery is dark and forbidding. For a while I am unsure where we are, but the hawk lifts me into the sky.

The sun begins to appear from behind the dusky clouds and we fly towards it. The light is more radiant now and we are flying very high. I seem to through a 90° shift as I ascend and feel almost two-dimensional. I now have to lift myself out of that vertical plane and face a gathering of people who are bathed in light.

I am with a gathering of spiritual devotees who are dressed in robes. An orange-golden light pervades the scene. At first I stand on the periphery. A man rides his horse into a large fire which is glowing in the centre of the group. He is unaffected

70

by it. Now I see a figure with four arms, moving in *mudras*, revealing spiritual motion. He has a distinctly Buddha-like appearance.

It is my turn. I have a 'baptism of fire' but am unscathed by the flames although they lap all around me. Looking down I see I am sitting on a silvery pentagram which seems to have a magnetic field effect — shielding me from the destructive power of the flames which billow all around in waves.

Now a new figure begins to dominate my vision. It is a deity with a hawk's head and a human body and seems to be related to my power animal. He is about to speak to me as Moses ceases drumming and I have to return . . .

For some time Moses had been interested in a technique he calls 'image taking'. If a paradoxical image presents itself during a guided imagery journey, the idea is for the practitioner to 're-conjure' it into consciousness, and almost become possessed by it, while other members of the group ask questions about its origin and purpose. Puzzled by the nature of the hawk-entity that had appeared at the end of my journey, I resolved to call it forth. I sat on the small chair that we had agreed should be the 'shaman's seat' and began to focus all my attention on actually *becoming* the mysterious bird-god. Moses and Ly began to ask me questions:

I tell them I am a bird-man. Moses askes me who I am. I answer:
I am Abraxas.
(This was truly extraordinary, because I had never made a conscious connection between the hawk-headed Abraxas and my magical hawk ally, although it seems obvious enough now)
I am an eagle with soaring, expansive wings who flies at the top of the vault of the universe, confined only by the curve of the sky. It is a great pressure for me to combine with a human form. I feel at times that the lower part of my body is constricted like a strait-jacket, a difference of densities between the cosmic sky and my ventures on the earth plane. (Now a moment which Moses later told me was sad and poignant . . .) I tell them I am losing my wings and becoming

71

more human. My body seems to constrict all over and I become sweaty and clammy . . .

Gradually I awake.

It was this journey, more than any other, that demonstrated that in reality a variety of magical techniques can lead towards the same regions of inner space. In essence, shamanic meditation and ritual drumming are guided imagery techniques which make full use of sensory deprivation. When external visual stimuli are cut off, it is quite normal for internal imagery to manifest in a compensatory manner, and if the venture inwards is specific enough — focused, for example, on the cosmic tree or magical flight — a universal layer of mythic imagery can be tapped.* What was happening now was that the range of symbols that I found personally meaningful was resurfacing in a new way. New casks for old wine . . .

The Gnostic content of the image-taking was also quite apparent. In the early Christian centuries many of the Gnostic sects had been accused of denying the body, and regarding it as evil. It seems to me that perhaps what was meant by this Gnostic teaching was precisely a question of 'densities'. In the Gnostic conception there were sacred realms of being and profane areas too, and a continuum existed between them. The Gnostics characterised the mystic quest as a venture towards the spirit and, symbolically, the gross vehicle of the body — with all its sensory restrictions — was comparatively less important. Our image-taking experiment seemed to show that pure spirit found it difficult to coexist with the much 'denser' level of human existence.

Shamanism was certainly providing a challenge, and posed as many questions as there were answers. In several respects, the journeys were also proving to be quite unpredictable. With

---

* See also John Lilly's *Centre of the Cyclone* and *Simulations of God* for material linking the sensory deprivation condition and personal belief systems.

hindsight I am sure that this was a good thing. We are all inclined to like our religious beliefs to be neatly packaged and enclosed — there is a type of security in being able to hold on to a body of religious concepts that for us represents 'ultimate certainty'. Shamanism did not provide that type of security. I was finding that it did not lead specifically *anywhere*; that sacred images from a wide range of cultures could appear at any time. Much of what I experienced was proving to be personally meaningful but there was something about each journey that kept one ever-watchful at the same time. I was constantly reminded of the Yaqui shaman Don Juan's conversation with Carlos Castaneda:

> 'For me the world is weird because it is stupendous, awesome, mysterious, unfathomable . . . you must learn to make every act count, since you are going to be here for only a short while; in fact, too short for witnessing all the marvels of it.'

CHAPTER SEVEN

Allies of Power

During the next six months I noticed that certain patterns would recur during the shaman sessions. Often, in my mind's eye, I would find myself thrust into exotic cultures, for example among African natives or Red Indians or initiatory bands of Aborigines. The shaman's drum, by association, was leading me into areas where the mythologies had been rich and diverse, a clear contrast to the barrenness of mythic thought in our computer-dominated western society.

Another quite distinct theme involved my being attacked or devoured, either by adversaries or by my power animals themselves. My crocodile, for example, usually showed his affection for me by eating me, but I would always find that inside his belly I felt protected and well armoured and not at all fragmented. It was if something in me had to be broken down before a more integrated magical persona could be established. As a result of this perhaps, I felt increasingly that I was going through a 'rebirth' process.

Three of my journeys involved quite vicious attacks that symbolically involved my 'death' but which, in a positive way, culminated with impressive visions of the power-hawk and a feeling of my own 're-emergence'.

The drumming is very effective tonight. I enter the tunnel immediately and am aware of thronging people. They are negroid . . . I am in Africa (Dahomey?). There are circular huts with thatched roofs and the ground is very dusty. Huge palm trees catch my attention, and one in particular seems to reach up into the sky. I climb it instinctively, feeling that my power animal must be up there.

Soon a hawk appears, turns around and lets me mount on her back. We fly, but I am too frightened to look down, and I wonder where we are going.

We have arrived — at the domain of a Giant Hawk, who towers far above me. I stand at its feet like a grovelling earthworm.

Now I become aware of huge sculptures, some of them Egyptian and portraying hawk-like images. Others are less distinct. They encircle me, in a manner similar to the monoliths at Stonehenge. A young assistant dressed in Egyptian-style clothing comes upon me with a cudgel and begins to beat me. I become pulp-like but feel no pain.

Now, as I lie upon the ground on my back, a female hawk flies down and rests gently on my genital area. There is no eroticism, but it seems to be some kind of sexual encounter. I feel I am being reborn as a young hawk. Energy courses into my arms and I feel them turning into wings. I rise, hawk-like, from my body.

The drumming ceases, and I return through the tunnel. I am pleased by tonight's adventure. It is good to re-establish a firm bond with the hawk.

* * *

My entry tonight is through a fireplace which includes as part of its design a decorative metal rim. I travel through a succession of arches filled with golden light but eventually come to a more hostile location where I am hemmed in by warriors.

Once again, the figures are African. They raise their spears menacingly in the air above me, as if I am some sort of sacrificial animal (a pig of some sort . . . ?). I let them spear me, but there is no feeling of pain.

My vision now switches to a Red Indian locale and I see a medicine-man performing a bird dance. Feathers adorn his hair and arms. Meanwhile I am told that I am a hawk and I should rise up from the carcass of the slain animal (the pig). I am instructed that in tribute I should bare my chest-wound to the sun, and allow its healing rays to fall upon the gash.

As the rays of sunlight warm my skin, a hand comes to view in the right side of my vision. It comes closer, and inserts a crystal into my body. I look down and see the crystal within, as if my body were hollow . . .

Now I rise up into the air and come to a mountainous domain where there are huge eagles and other birds of prey, much, much bigger than I. I see their heads clearly silhouetted against the bright blue sky and they are awesome to behold . . . Are they comrades of Abraxas?

* * *

The drumming begins and I have no trouble entering the tunnel. I come out in a grove of trees which fills the sky with branches and foliage, allowing only occasional glimpses of blue sky.

I come to a tree with a very straight trunk, and begin to climb upwards. The tree resembles an elongated silver birch. After climbing for a short time I come to a 'jungle' (It doesn't occur to me at the time how preposterous this is!) where I notice a dark-skinned crocodile frothing around in some marshy reeds. It seems smaller than other power-crocodiles I have encountered but it soon makes its presence felt by beginning to devour me, feet first. I allow him to do this, feeling no pain, and when I am inside his belly I feel protected and strong, as if encased in firm leather armour. I have to continue up the tree, however, so I cut myself out of his belly with a dagger, and begin once again to climb vertically.

I become aware of a pair of amber-orange eyes, and then the beak and visage of my bird of prey. It begins to peck at my throat, gradually dismembering me until I become a ball, and then an egg. The bird then sits over me, and I have the feeling that I have to fight to be 'hatched'. At times I seem to be under the nest as well as under the bird . . . almost as if I have to battle my way up on to its level. I gradually emerge from the egg and notice as I peer over the nest-rim that other bird-men warriors are up there too — and they are dancing.

I become bird-like, and float off into the sky. I am not able to see clearly below, however, and my last impressions before the drumming ceases, are of the wind and a hazy blue light.

It is good to reaffirm my links with my power animals. When they eat me, I know they like me!

Two subsequent sessions revealed interesting aspects of the symbol of the totem pole which is, of course, a form of the mythological 'world axis' that unites the different worlds or planes of the shaman's journey:

At first I am not sure where I am, but gradually I become aware of a luxuriant orchard filled with citrus trees. A crystalline river flows through the orchard and its surface has a remarkable mirror-like sheen. I am somewhat surprised, but not unduly alarmed, when a crocodile comes towards me, showing itself four times to me. I have met it before, on other occasions.

The crocodile opens its jaws wide and I sit inside its mouth and cruise down the placid river as if in a small boat. There are figures dancing on the bank and they become increasingly dominant in my field of vision. The figures are leaping and dancing with amazingly slow, graceful motions, as if they are gravity-free. They then form into a column, standing upon each other's shoulders, and form a human totem pole. I rise up the pole, high into the misty blue sky, and for a time the journey seems endless.

Now a large Red Indian stands before me and I look very clearly into his eyes. He sings a chant, which becomes abstract and rhythmic: 'ne, ne, ne . . . ' It is the first time I recall hearing sound from within the visionary sequence itself, during a shamanic exercise.

It is raining on the roof of the house where we are and this seems to influence the nature of the inner journey.

The scene becomes dark and menacing, and rain begins to fall heavily within my vision also. Through steely-grey pellets of rain I discern the supremely 'central' and pivotal image of a great eagle-hawk and I look deeply into his right eye, which shines with a green-yellow glow. His feathers glisten dark brown, and his presence — as always — is quite awesome.

I float back down, entering a Red Indian wigwam from the top. It feels protective, almost womb-like. Then as the rapid drumming commences, I return to the room where the journey began.

* * *

I do the drumming myself this evening but I find, to my surprise, that I can still enter the shamanic world; my drumming does not interfere.

I am with a band of Aborigines. I see them very clearly. Their dark skins glisten as they sit around the campfire and there are white daubs of paint on their foreheads and cheeks.

The figures are in a circle but soon they transform into a human chain, like a centipede, and in turn become a crocodile which chases its own tail (like the alchemical dragon). The form of the crocodile, reinforced by the drum-beat, creates a circular entry-point and I travel through the tunnel that has been created, into a region of watery depths.

The waters part around me as I travel, and I feel rather like the Biblical Moses, parting the waves as I move along.

Now it has become dark and I am surrounded by a group of native shamans. This time they are not Aborigines, but Red Indians.

As I watch, the chief of the band, who is resplendent in a feathered head-dress, stands up and his head — minus his body — seems to ascend a totem pole. I rise up with him, and meet various rather solemn Indians whom I take to be ancestor spirits although I am not given their names. I anticipate meeting my hawk, but it is not to be. At the top of the pole is my crocodile's mouth. I am swallowed whole and come back down *inside* the totem pole!

I am back in a domain of watery textures and diffuse light. My last impression is of a light-bearing messenger riding towards me on a horse. There is no specific communication but he does not seem hostile. The quality of the light is very unusual and a sort of yellow incandescence rises from the ground.

Now I stop the drumming and return through a pool of water to the room where we had begun.

I am impressed that the magical journey can also operate while one is drumming oneself. The activity becomes automatic after a while and does not intrude after all.

In November 1981 I noticed that the imagery from the western occult tradition was entering the shaman visions more distinctly. This tendency has since continued, perhaps not surprisingly.

An example of this 'parallel symbolism' occurred when the symbol of the Holy Grail appeared on one of the journeys. However shamanism and western magic and mysticism all involve personal transformation as part of the quest, and the Holy Grail is one such metaphor for the spiritual journey. The symbol of the cup — which at different times is the womb of the Great Mother or the cup of the spirit of life — is present in both orthodox Christian mysticism and the occult mythology of the Tarot. I also began to find that in a shamanic context it had the same type of meaning:

> We have a guest drummer tonight. Carmen has begun to drum after putting us all through an excellent progressive relaxation. Rose essence wafts through the air from an incense stick.
>
> My initial intention is to travel downwards through the root system of the tree I have visualised. However the entire journey proves to be a rising through various planes within the hollow trunk of the tree. Initially I am in a ground-level chamber similar to our room in the house.
>
> Immediately my mind is dominated by the image of Red Indians dancing in a circle, their feather head-dresses uplifted in the breeze. I rise, bird-like, above them, and find myself approaching a ceiling of cloud. Having passed through it, I begin to dance like a bird myself, and gradually realise that I am in a large teepee. I look up and see what seems to be a disc of light, visible through the apex. I travel up towards it, and now encounter one of my two power animals: the crocodile.
>
> I am rapidly engulfed by a chaotic slurring of crocodile images but they transform into a mandala of crocodiles, all

with their snouts facing the centre. Out of this focal area arises a large, Grail-like cup filled with silver light.

It rises slowly into the air and I follow it. I find myself summoning my hawk ally. I can only see the hawk dimly at first. Then I have the feeling of reaching a mountain peak and flying through the air gracefully at an enormous height. I am only vaguely aware of the valleys and rivers far below me but I return to the peak and am aware that the hawk has human characteristics — primeval and unfamiliar.

The hawk becomes even more human and a golden light emerges from his chest. I have a strong impression of an Egyptian figure, perhaps a priest, waiting nearby. The light now solidifies into the form of a golden goblet, and as I watch, the hawk dissolves into it gradually. The Egyptian priest, solemn and dignified, remains in the background as the hawk's head disappears.

It is an impressive and mysterious sight. I have the sensation of being bathed in golden light myself — somehow it has poured down on top of me — and then the drumming summons me back. I find it difficult to return. It has been a most enjoyable and literally 'elevating' experience.

Unfortunately, the pattern of regular shaman meetings became disrupted at this stage. Ly was finding strong parallels between shamanism and Wicca, and was being urged by members of her coven to spend more time with them. Moses, meanwhile, returned to his earlier role as a solitary magician in the urban wilderness.

For a while, to my regret, shamanism was relegated to a minor role in my activities. It was difficult working alone because even though one could drum for oneself, it required a lot more concentration and was best shared by the group.

However the shaman sessions were able to begin again in November 1982 — primarily as a result of a chance encounter with two like-minded occultists whom I had not met before.

CHAPTER EIGHT

Towards Abraxas

Several years earlier, while researching a book on occult sects, I had met a 'goddess worshipper' named Marguerite Moor. Marguerite had established a unique magical group called the Order of Isis-Ishtar in a north shore suburb of Sydney and it attracted many different types of people: marketing managers, accountants, students, waitresses, labourers and radical feminists — all of them interested in learning more about the feminine side of their inner nature. Marguerite combined mythology, Tarot, astrology and ritual in her Order and had nine grades encompassing many different forms of the Universal Goddess. These included Geshtinanna, the Mesopotamian goddess of wine and grapes; Cybele, the Titan earth goddess; Astarte and Isis, the Phoenician and Egyptian goddesses of fertility, and Venus/Aphrodite, the classical goddess of beauty and love.

One afternoon, at Marguerite's request, I held a shaman gathering in her temple for members of her Order. After I had explained the techniques, they began to dance around a candle in the centre of the temple floor, while I drummed from the periphery. Many of them had immediate impressions as they began to dance their power animals. One woman had an eagle, others had wild cats and one man had the front half of an elephant (two legs only!). The second dance proved more effective. This time the elephant manifested in its complete form, one girl discovered she had a Bengal Tiger for

83

an ally, and there were two snakes — a boa constrictor and a cobra — both of them incarnating in very petite females. One man discovered that he had a snail as his power animal, something I hadn't encountered before. He rejected it outright as a magical ally and insisted that it depart from his vision, but it declined, and he had to accept it. Among other power animals that appeared were a black panther and a wolf.

It was a successful first venture into shamanic practice for the group, who were already well trained in visualisation. Marguerite told me that she would invite me to a 'ritual feast', to be held soon, to meet the participants in a more casual environment. Marguerite was holding these meetings to encourage members of her Order to meet occultists working in other traditions, and she was keen to diffuse the sense of secrecy that was present in most occult groups.

Robert and Ian — two young occultists who would be my partners in shamanism later on — were discussing Aleister Crowley's magical system with Marguerite's Order members when I first met them. Interested in Crowley's sacramental approach to magic, and his diverse body of writings, Robert and Ian were involved in establishing a Kabbalistic research centre and also — as I later discovered — had the largest filing system on international metaphysical and occult groups that I had ever seen. We soon discovered a mutual interest in trance magic, and agreed to meet again as soon as possible — in order to exchange techniques and information.

Although their flat was comparatively small, Robert and Ian had put one room aside for ritual workings. There was a metal-frame pyramid on the floor, one or two crystal pendants appropriate for ceremonial (but also strikingly similar to shamanic power objects) and several mattresses and cushions to lie on while embarking on the mind-journeys. There was also a complete hi-fi stereo system to allow us to play electronic music as an accompaniment. I had recently obtained a cassette of Michael Harner's shaman drumming from a mail order company in Big Sur, and was anxious to try

84

it as an alternative to actual drumming. The tape proved to be very effective indeed and had the advantage of running for 25 minutes on each side — at two different drum beats, fast and slow. I had found in our earlier shaman sessions that few of us could sustain a regular drum-beat for more than fifteen minutes and of course this was a restriction on the length of the journeys.

Our first meeting together produced excellent results. We positioned ourselves in turn beneath the metal-frame pyramid, which even seemed symbolically appropriate — a technological equivalent of the Red Indian teepee and the tomb of the Pharoahs . . . Using the cassette tape of the drumming in the intimacy of a small, darkened room proved to be quite as effective as the actual drum. We each took turns and recorded a written account of the journeys afterwards. I was pleased that, despite a gap of several months, my magical allies had not deserted me:

> I feel a strong sensation of bright, geometric lights and pulsing energy and lie back on the mattress beneath the metal frame. I summon the cosmic tree and begin immediately to become my hawk. I am very aware of my heavy wings, propelling me through the air. The drumming is on 'slow beat' rather than on rapid. I fly over numerous snow-clad mountains, above pine forests, and into a grey misty twilight. At times I seem to be perched on top of a high mountain peak surveying the night-sky. The drum does not particularly propel me tonight, and at times it contains, rather than releases me . . . almost like driving nails into a coffin. This has an interesting shamanic affect, because of the task of constructing a new spirit body! A river of silver crystal begins to pour over me, making me a new body. I become very aware of the drumming and it is as if nails are being hammered into my body, not to harm me but to reconstruct my form. I breathe deeply, and new vigour and life comes into my new body . . .
>
> Now I can fly again, and through the forest I come to a huge mansion-like dwelling, half concealed by snow. The mansion itself is mountain-like, and drawn through one of the

Justice

illumined windows, I come towards a silvery light source and look upwards.

A sacred being is seated on a throne. At first I wonder if it is a lunar form of Thoth — the deity looks Egyptian and is seated rather stolidly on a throne in the manner of the large Egyptian sculptures. The head, at first glance looks Ibis-like, but as I draw closer I see that it is more the form of a crocodile. I observe it first in profile but its snout becomes more prominent and I know now that I will have to submit myself to it, as I have done with my power animal before. Its teeth are sharp filaments, more delicate than the teeth of a real crocodile, but I manage not to be frightened. As the snout comes towards me I see that the god is offering me a single lustrous pearl. Taking the gift, I lie in its mouth and its snout closes, holding me. I do not panic, but feel new assurance and confidence.

The drumming continues and again I am travelling over snow and dark forest. I sense that I am drawing near to the domain of a snow-queen and look for her form in the light before me. Her eyes and hair are jagged with icicles and frost and there is a steely-grey light radiating from her body. She tells me her name is Sedna, and I have seen her before beneath the waves of an angry sea. Now she takes on aspects which remind me of the Tarot card *Justice*. She holds a steel sword above me which at first seems very threatening — almost like the sword of Damocles. But this then becomes the central axis for a pair of scales and I see that she is judging me. I sway back and forth beneath her and then I feel I am becoming a young child, rocking in her arms. The sense of peace and comfort is wonderful and reassuring.

The drumming ceases and I return.

This journey had certain qualities which distinguished it from those which had preceded it. For the first time a quite particular archetype from the Tarot — the goddess of the *Justice* trump — had appeared in a shamanic context. I was also responding to the drumming in new ways, and learning that the drum-beat could be both a propelling and an inhibiting force, both of them appropriate in different symbolic situations.

On several occasions I have found my body being re-structured in a mythic sense, and often the rhythmic drum-beats have seemed to be the hammerings of a deity at work. The formation of a magical body was one of the sequences on the next visionary journey:

I ascend in a column of smoke which billows upwards from a camp-fire. Looking down I can see that I am rising quite high in the sky. Once again I have become immersed in a stream of liquid crystals which shine and twinkle with silver light. I am shown how the gods — it seems to be Thor specifically — fashion shamans from the quartz rock.

I can see a man's chest, and then other parts of his torso, being sculpted from the crystalline rock-face on the side of a cliff. A person emerges from the rock. Now I realise it is me!

But as I stand free of the rock I feel much shorter than I really am and realise that I am without a head!

Paradoxically, this isn't at all alarming. I am now given a crystalline head to complete my body structure, and this is fitted to me almost like a medieval helmet.

I come now to a Red Indian teepee (the dramatic change of cultures seems quite natural at the time) where a figure is dancing. Bird feathers adorn his arms and body. There is a sense of the Indian being me also. I am caught up in the dance, which is clearly totemic. My body changes its proportions and I begin to acquire an animal form. I have a long, muscular abdomen and short, lizard-like legs. Then, as I contemplate my form, I realise that I am dancing my crocodile!

It is a strange sensation: primeval and atavistic, with all the impressions of a lower animal intelligence but also a strong and vital force in Nature.

The teepee has become a crystalline pyramid and, as I look upwards, I notice chunks of crystal falling upon the pyramid like heavy rain. A totem pole forms within the teepee, and I rise up. As I do so, I ask to see my other power animal . . .

I summon strong images of the hawk, and then see it seated on the top of the pyramid, which by now has become a mountain. The hawk has its back to me, and I prepare to mount it.

Instead I *become* the hawk, and as I merge with its body I am surprised by the sheer weight of the creature's wings as I endeavour to fly slowly through the air.

I now ask for a gift from my hawk, and we seem to separate. I am presented with what looks initially like small mussels. I then see that inside one of the shells, which must be oysters after all, is a bright, luminescent white pearl. The symbolism of the shell is impressed upon me . . . the hard protective surface of the shell housing the precious gift within.

The drum has stopped and with some reluctance I return to the room.

The renewed discipline of meeting regularly for shamanic journeys was obviously a positive factor. We were all finding the experiences to be rich in mythic imagery. For my part, the initiatory rebirth themes, the allusions to the Tarot archetypes, and the sense of participating in a new type of magical reality, continued with each meeting:

December 9

At first I feel surrounded by evil, predatory forces. A large crab-like monster fills the sky as I endeavour to rise up in the smoke of the campfire. I see an Indian chief conjuring over the flames but he looks ominous. He is wearing a horned feather head-dress and stares out at me with dark, pitted eyes. I feel drawn into the fire, but yield to it rather than become frightened . . . knowing that I should not panic. For a while I seem to float above myself . . . a sense of dissociation.

The sky has now become a dull amorphous brown colour but eventually opens up, as a tunnel of silver light forms in the dark murkiness above me. I call to my hawk to free me and find myself able to stretch vertically. However, the drumming seems to be nailing my feet to the ground, and I am unable to pass through the tunnel.

The scenery now changes so that I come to resemble a Jack-and-the-Beanstalk figure. I have become a huge giant traversing the heavens. Now there is another switch, and I have become microscopically small, standing beside the ankle of a huge giant who towers above me. The symbolism of the giant now disappears as I myself become the World Tree, heavily ornamented with diverse and very intricate 'universal' motifs. As I contemplate the complex beauty and grandeur of the Tree my perspective changes so that I perceive the huge axial trunk stretching upwards from my chest into the heavens, while roots come out of my back, reaching down into the earth. I am literally 'middle earth', extending horizontally in all directions: a most bizarre sensation!

I have become like liquid soil. Someone is stirring me, and I realise I am in a bubbling cauldron. The image of *Temperance* comes to mind immediately. My texture has become viscous. I am clinging to the stirring stick like a cacoon to a branch. My body meanwhile is changing shape. My crocodile is there to eat me also (as he always does!) and my form begins to break down into diffuse elements . . .

Now there is a distinct change. I experience a soaring effect as I become a knight in dark armour riding a white, winged horse. I am seeking the Holy Grail. I rise up the side of a mountain and can see a cross superimposed on top of it. The mountain — Calvary — is illuminated, and Christ-like, I find myself being crucified. There is a definite sense of detachment to this experience — no impression of passionate involvement . . .

I call for my power hawk but feel he has forsaken me. No vision of the Grail presents itself either. Meanwhile the drumming has ended but I know that I have not resolved my situation. I ask Robert and Ian to let me continue by turning the drum cassette over to the other side.

(Slow drum-beat cassette)

The Hermit

I have come to another mountain. There is a heavy blizzard and deep snowdrifts hug the rocks. I see a dark, silhouetted figure ahead of me. He is hidden in a cloak and his face is not visible, but he has a lamp to guide him up the treacherous mountain path; I recognise him as *The Hermit.*

I merge with his form and feel I am being taken to meet 'The Goddess'. However, I do not see her fully; her down-stretched hand reaches towards me but her face is not visible.

Now my attention focuses on the drum-beat and my vision is dominated by the texture of wood. I am shown 'The Drum' (an archetypal shaman's drum) and merge with its shape. It encompasses me like a womb.

My body, once again, seems to dissolve. It is totally liquid, without form. The rapid four-fold drum signal summons me back. Still I feel that the journey is unresolved, but has been preparatory for something else . . . perhaps initiatory.

Something deep is stirring in me. I am re-forming. My essence is being channelled towards a new expression.

* * *

December 17

My first visual impression is of a giant eagle, perched majestically on the top of a mountain, sedately surveying the world below. He seems loft, distant, immovable. I am given his name: *Abraxas* . . .

Now I see a number of people bowing reverently to the earth. There are several intense points of light shining on the ground. They are luminescent pearls that give off radiation like laser beams and their colour changes from green through to purple. The people are awestruck by these marvellous power objects.

An imposing figure now stands before me. He reminds me of *The Hierophant* from Aleister Crowley's pack except that a large, all-seeing eye emanates from his chest, replacing the pentagram.

I am led into a large initiatory hall, whose vaulted ceiling rises high into the sky. Huge Egyptian gods in close formation

91

tower above me. It is as if I am an ant surveying a huge mural that has come alive. I recognise Thoth and Isis, and an alligator-headed god whom I later learn is Sebek-Ra, a form of the dark god Set.

The ceiling of the temple now seems to dissolve into blue sky as the sun rises in the distance. We are all bathed in warm sunlight but the sun itself is not visible.

January 21

As the drumming begins I rise up in the curls of smoke, I open my wings as I take the form of the hawk. Before me, in my focused vision, I can see a crystalline shape forming: it becomes a geometric, stylised mountain. I fly towards it in the greyish night sky.

I am shown a beautiful naked woman who seems to be enclosed in an alchemical type of flask — she is moving around inside it. At the same time, I am strongly aware of the beating drum, which seems to be the very pulse of life itself. I can feel its vibrancy in my body like an enhanced heartbeat and for a brief moment I become the drum.

What has been the crystal mountain now becomes the central pillar of the Tree of Life, except that it is formed of entwined human components — muscle, sections of the abdomen, the breast and so on. As I rise up, it becomes a tunnel and I have the impression that it is the birth canal and I am becoming foetus-like. I am going to give birth to myself! My foetal body includes my power animals: I have images of the hawk and the crocodile, and also an elephant . . . which is new to me. All of these are somehow combined.

For a while I seem to be plunging into an evil morass; a slimey devil with tentacles lurks around trying to engulf me, but I laugh at him and he dissolves. The scene lightens immediately . . . there seems to be an aspect of confronting one's *karma* here . . .

As the drumming continues I feel the undulatory movements of a woman giving birth, although there is no sensation of pain (perhaps, because as a man, this is outside my range of experience). At times, as if from the viewpoint of the mother, I look down at my enlarged abdomen as if expecting the child to be born.

The sun is rising through the clouds, bringing the journey to a climax, but somehow I withdraw from going through the birth experience. At the end, the journey is unresolved, but nevertheless has strong initiatory implications. I am beginning to realise that the shamanic journey combines both magical *will*, but also *the capacity to surrender to a higher process*. I suspect I am holding back on this . . .

Nevertheless, I feel very peaceful and relaxed after the journey.

The shamanic vision quest had now reached an interesting point. The Gnostic deity Abraxas had become clearly identified with my hawk ally in my own personal mythology. I was also finding quite remarkable fusions between the Tarot imagery, which had been part of my world for so long, and the rich and universal symbolism of shamanic rebirth. And, increasingly, the inner journey of the spirit was becoming an encounter with the abstract and infinite qualities of the Cosmos:

I raise my arms upwards as the drumming begins, and feel myself lifting away. I am becoming the eagle-hawk; my wings are extended and I am flying. Now I find I am becoming an egg. A shell encloses me and I feel I must break through . . .

Tonight I feel very fluid, as if I am surrounded by vibrant waves of energy. It is very astral and more abstract than usual. I have the strong feeling of the shaman's role to break through different planes of being.

I rise up out of the egg, a young eagle emerging into flight for the first time. I am very aware now of a dark god standing before me and feel it is a test of strength. The god is a dark form of Horus, and his black hawk eyes look at me piercingly. This negative god now becomes Baphomet, sinister and evil, but I am not frightened of him. Gradually his form dissolves and a silver pentagram replaces him.

I am now transforming myself by amalgamating the four elements. From being fluid, light and airy, I become dense and rock-like. I feel there is a shell or enclosing surface to break through into a different reality.

My clarity of vision improves and I am drawing very close to my two power animals. I see the head of my giant hawk extremely close: the texture of the feathers on the head in minute detail, the eye in profile. I merge with the hawk, but find as I do so that it now becomes a crocodile as well. My body becomes strong and armoured, and I can feel the tail moving. I am dense and heavily structured.

The drumming becomes more noticeable and somehow I am aware that I must be born in a new form which encompasses my power animals. I see a foetus swimming in blue fluid, and it feels as if I am in an oceanic womb. Then I become increasingly smaller and the sense of space dominates.

My field of vision becomes an exquisite and intense blue. There are thousands of people here, worshipping a force in the heavens. The sky tints with gold and it is very awesome, at times reminiscent of the Tarot trump *Judgment* except that a drum rather than a trumpet heralds the presence of a great god.

I look upwards and the azure blue sky seems to take a vault-like shape, like the ceiling of a great cathedral. I am in the domain of Abraxas but he is mysterious and elusive.

I call his name and I see a huge hawk, but one thing is puzzling: he has no face. He seems to flow into infinity . . . He is the 'bornless one'.

Once again I have a feeling of the enormity of space, and the strong impression that the magical journey itself, rather than any specific goal, is the important thing.

It is very Zen-like.

Abraxas is the hawkless-hawk, the God-who-is-not.

A form of space.

It still seems very remarkable to me that archetypes from an essentially forgotten religion like Gnosticism can reappear in one's consciousness.

Whether my concept of Abraxas is comparable to Jung's, or even to that of the third century Gnostic mystics, is hard to judge. Nevertheless, from the very beginnings of my journey through magic and occultism, the symbolism of Abraxas has had special appeal for me. More than any other deity I have been aware of, Abraxas represents the polar opposites of consciousness and therefore seems to me to be a much more complete deity than one who is specifically good or evil. If I have learned anything from magic, it is that the path ideally leads to a state of inner balance, and that means integrating both the positive and negative forces of the psyche.

In the final analysis, shamanism and visionary magic both lead to a similar place. It has been called the 'separate reality', the 'crack between the worlds', the sacred ground where self-initiation occurs. What is most remarkable of all, is that the old gods are still accessible, and are still there to help us on the journey.

CHAPTER NINE

A Final Note . . .

This book really has no ending, for the shamanic quest itself is an ongoing process.

I am convinced that the shaman's journey, in a very real and personal way, is a pathway to sacred space. In many so-called 'primitive' societies, such a concept would be familiar enough, for here the myths and deities associated with creation, fertility, and birth and death, are alive as a function of everyday life.

In our somewhat clinical, and some would say alienating, modern society, access to the sacred and awesome areas of being is harder to come by. Some have found this type of mystical experience through a church, others through meditation or through psychedelic states of consciousness. It seems to me that one should refrain from passing judgement on whether one path is superior to, or more appropriate than, another. In the final analysis we are all seeking a personal mythology, a framework of meaning which encompasses not only the complex realities of modern life but also the abstract and intangible realms of our inner being.

The path to the sacred introduces us to profound areas of meaning. We begin to understand our place within the cyclical and universal processes of Nature and — perhaps for the first time — we are able to participate in the mythologies that have enriched our culture centuries before we were born.

Shamanism is very much an adventure of the spirit and, for me, its fascination is endless. One can hardly say more than that.

Collage by Nevill Drury

APPENDIX A

Inner Space Music for use with Guided Imagery

The growth of the genre

One of the offshoots of the psychedelic period of the late 1960s and early 1970s was the emergence of textural synthesiser music. Much of this music was ideally suited to the altered states of consciousness produced by hallucinogenic drugs and meditation.

British rock groups like Pink Floyd, King Crimson and Hawkwind pioneered this approach, initially with complex compositions that made full use of electrical guitar and synthesiser effects to support their vocals. However, from the viewpoint of guided imagery work, the later development of electronic 'cosmic rock' music is of more interest. The lyrics gradually receded in importance and the musicians concentrated on producing abstract music where the full impact of the texture and colour could be experienced to the full.

The German group Tangerine Dream, comprising Edgar Froese, Peter Baumann and Cristoph Franke produced some remarkable albums in the early 1970s which remain classics in the cosmic rock genre. Their early albums for the Ohr label in Berlin included *Zeit, Alpha Centauri* and *Atem*, and these recordings, together with two for the British Virgin label — *Phaedra* and *Rubycon* — are still among the most notable examples of 'inner space' music. The compositions had an

Pioneering cosmic rock band King Crimson. Guitarist Robert Fripp has since worked with other 'inner space' musicians, like Brian Eno
Courtesy: Island and Festival Records

eerie loneliness and were permeated by an ethereal, supernatural quality. Much of their later music, for example that on the live *Encore* double album, and on *Force Majeure* and *Stratosfear*, has proved to be much more rhythmic and, in large degree, less transcendental.

The other major group of the early German period was Ash Ra Tempel, a group that had performed live with Timothy Leary at the Berne Festival, on Walpurgis Night, 1972. Their keyboards player, Klaus Schulze, who studied Liszt, Debussy and Stockhausen, as well as progressive rock, has since produced a number of remarkable solo albums for the Brain-Metronome and Ohr labels in Germany, and Virgin and Island in Britain. Outstanding examples of his work, from a 'mind-journey' point of view, are the intricate *Mirage* album, which includes the beautiful composition 'Crystal Lake', and the earlier recordings *Irrlicht, Blackdance* and *Moondawn*.

Ash Ra Tempel also included in its lineup the superb guitarist Manuel Gottsching, who now records both under his own name and as Ash Ra. His albums *Inventions for Electrical Guitar* and *New Age of Earth*, both have excellent individual tracks, without sustaining a meditative mood throughout.

In recent years European electronic music has become more rhythmic, and, in the case of Jean-Michel Jarré and Vangelis, more melodic. The 'inner space' quality of the earlier European recordings seems to be receding as a fashion.

In Britain a number of musicians emerged in the 1970s as leading exponents of experimental synthesiser and acoustic music, including Mike Oldfield, the two-man group Jade Warrior, and Brian Eno — formerly of Roxy Music. Eno also appears in several 'combinations', for example with Robert Fripp and Harold Budd. His so-called 'ambient' albums on the EG label are outstanding examples of inner space mood music. Mike Oldfield, always more rhythmic and melodic than Brian Eno, has produced several notable and varied albums including *Ommadawn*, *Incantations* and his best known work *Tubular Bells*, which provided the theme music for *The Exorcist*.

For a long time synthesiser music was comparatively unpopular in the United States although isolated musicians like Terry Riley tried their hand at it. Riley's music lacked the subtlety of the best European albums, but in recent years there has been a resurgence of electronic and acoustic mood music on the west coast, led by Steven Halpern, Robert Bearns, Ron Dexter and the flautist Larkin. Halpern describes the genre as the 'anti-frantic alternative' — music for relaxation and self-healing. The Canadian Paul Horn has also produced a number of outstanding flute albums which have a pure and relaxing mystical quality. These include *Inside* (recorded within the chambers of the Taj Mahal) and *Inside the Great Pyramid*, its Egyptian equivalent. This trend still continues. Several artists are producing delicate acoustic albums in the United States for the Sri Rajneesh organisation, and Japanese musician Kitaro, who has been influenced by Klaus Schulze, now combines a variety of instruments on his albums, including synthesiser, guitar and percussion. His recordings are released both in the United States and Germany.

Application in guided imagery work

Magical pathworkings, guided imagery journeys and mind-games of the type evolved by Robert Masters and Jean Houston, often benefit from the use of accompanying, non-intrusive music. The texture and quality of the music should be carefully considered so that it complements the symbolic nature of the inner visualisation. The magical tradition lends itself well to this type of application. Many of its images derive from the medieval concept of a universe consisting of four elements: earth, water, fire and air. The range of electronic effects is now so vast that one can draw on the genre for specific tracks to enhance this type of visual imagery. The music is best played in the background, allowing the guide to read over it to members of the group. The mind journey that I conducted at the Transpersonal Conference in 1980 (see Chapter Four) was based on the symbolism of the Middle Pillar of the Kabbalistic Tree of Life and involved Tarot paths encompassing the elements earth, water and fire. I have found a combination of Klaus Schulze's composition 'Crystal Lake' and Edgar Foese's 'Maroubra Bay' to be especially supportive of the symbolic mood of this journey. The text of this pathworking is more practical than the much longer 22-path Tarot journey included in my earlier work *Don Juan, Mescalito and Modern Magic*. In 1979 I produced an experimental tape of that guided imagery sequence and combined it with synthesiser and acoustic music*. The following amalgamation is just one example of numerous possible variants, but it shows how this type of music can be used to support the mood of individual pathworkings:

---

* This tape was purely experimental and was for my own personal use only. It cannot be marketed or distributed for obvious reasons of copyright.

Tarot Trump	Accompanying Music
The World	'Granchester Meadows' from Pink Floyd: *Ummagumma*; 'Ways of Changes' from Klaus Schulze: *Blackdance*
Judgement	'Why?' from Herbert Joos: *Daybreak*
The Moon	'Epsilon in Malaysian Pale' from Edgar Froese's album of the same name; 'Part Seven' from Pink Floyd: *Wish You Were Here*
The Sun	'Force Majeure' (last third only) from Tangerine Dream's album of the same name
The Star	'Mindphaser' from Klaus Schulze: *Moondawn*; 'Crystal Lake' from Klaus Schulze: *Mirage*
The Tower	'The Flood' from Lol Creme and Kevin Godley: *Consequences*
The Devil	'Rubycon Part One', from Tangerine Dream: *Rubycon*
Death	'Through Metamorphic Rocks' from Tangerine Dream: *Force Majeure*
Temperance	'Qasarsphere' from Manuel Gottsching: *Inventions for Electrical Guitar*
The Hanged Man	'Wind on Water' from Fripp & Eno: *Evening Star*
Justice	(as for preceding path 'The Hanged Man', flowing on)
Wheel of Fortune	'Theme Three' from Colosseum: *Valentyne Suite*

The Hermit	'Rubycon Part Two' (first third) from Tangerine Dream: *Rubycon*
Strength	'Rubycon Part Two' (middle section) from Tangerine Dream: *Rubycon*
The Charioteer	'Rubycon Part One' from Tangerine Dream: *Rubycon*
The Lovers	'Epsilon in Malaysian Pale' from Edgar Froese's album of the same name
The Hierophant	(as for preceding path, 'The Lovers', flowing on)
The Emperor	'Third Movement' from Tangerine Dream: *Zeit*
The Empress	(as for preceding path, 'The Emperor', flowing on)
The High Priestess	'Ocean of Tenderness' from Manuel Gottsching/Ash Ra: *New Age of Earth*
The Magician	(as for preceding path, 'The High Priestess', flowing on)
The Fool	'Qasarsphere' from Manuel Gottsching: *Inventions for Electrical Guitar*

Musical tastes, of course, vary considerably and the range of cosmic and meditative music available ranges from dramatic and intense synthesiser music through to bland and intricate background effects. The following is a selection of music that might be helpful for guided imagery work. I have classified the albums according to the dominant mood on the majority of tracks, but some albums obviously have a varied presentation. Personal experimentation for individual effects will be needed to arrive at the best combination for any particular pathworking: (Albums are listed alphabetically by artist, not necessarily in order of preference)

Music suggesting Space and Cosmos

Film Soundtrack	*2001: A Space Odyssey* (vocal tracks), MGM
Fripp & Eno	*Evening Star*, Island
Edgar Froese	*Aqua*, Virgin
Klaus Schulze	*Irrlicht*, Ohr
	Cyborg, Ohr
	Timewind, Virgin
	Blackdance, Virgin
Tangerine Dream	*Alpha Centauri*, Ohr
	Zeit, Ohr
	Phaedra, Virgin
	Rubycon, Virgin

Music of Intensity and Texture

Robert Bearns & Ron Dexter	*Golden Voyage* (3 vols.), Awakening Productions
Brian Eno	*On Land*, EG/Polydor
Jan Garbarek	*Dis*, ECM
Jade Warrior	*Waves*, Island
Laraaji	*Days of Radiance*, EG/Polydor
Herbie Mann	*Gaguku and Beyond*, Finnadar
Mike Oldfield	*Incantations*, Virgin
Klaus Schulze	*Moondawn*, Brain-Metronome
	Mirage, Island
Tangerine Dream	*Force Majeure*, Virgin

Music of Beauty and Simplicity

Ash Ra	*New Age of Earth*, Virgin

Ash Ra Tempel	*Join Inn*, Ohr
Harold Budd & Brian Eno	*The Plateaux of Mirror*, EG/Polydor
Brian Eno	*Discreet Music*, Antilles *Music for Airports*, EG/Polydor
Edgar Froese	*Epsilon in Malaysian Pale*, Virgin
Steven Halpern	*Zodiac Suite*, Halpern
Paul Horn	*Inside*, Epic *Inside the Great Pyramid*, Mushroom
Kitaro	*Oasis*, Kuckuck
Larkin	*Inner Sanctum*, Celestial Octaves

Music in which rhythm is dominant

Edgar Froese	*Ages*, Virgin
Manuel Gottsching	*Inventions for Electrical Guitar*, Ohr
Michael Hoenig	*Departure from the Northern Wasteland*, WB
Jean-Michel Jarré	*Equinox*, Polydor *Oxygene*, Polydor
Mike Oldfield	*Ommadawn*, Virgin
Klaus Schulze	*Bodylove*, Island
Tangerine Dream	*Encore*, Virgin *Stratosfear*, Virgin

Miscellaneous

Colosseum	*Valentyne Suite*, Fontana
Lol Creme & Kevin Godley	*Consequences*, Mercury
Herbert Joos	*Daybreak*, Japo

Mike Oldfield	*Tubular Bells*, Virgin
Pink Floyd	*Meddle*, Harvest
	Ummagumma, Harvest
	Wish You Were Here, Harvest
Terry Riley	*Shri Camel*, CBS
Vangelis	*Chariots of Fire*, Polydor
	Ignacio, Egg
Henry Wolff & Nancy Hennings	*Tibetan Bells II*, Celestial Harmonies

(*Note:* an excellent annotated guide to inner space music has recently been compiled by Anna Turner and Stephen Hill. Based on a selection of music played on the Berkeley, California radio station KPFA - FM during the last ten years, it is a very useful resource guide. Its title is *The Hearts of Space Guide*, PO Box 31321, San Francisco CA 94131).

Appendix B

Organisations and Groups

The following are contact addresses for groups and publications specialising in magical, shamanic and sacramental activities and research:

Magic Servants of the Light (SOL): PO Box 215, St Helier, Jersey, The Channel Islands

Circle: PO Box 219, Mt Horeb, Wisconsin 53572, USA

Shamanism Dr Michael Harner, Center for Shamanic Studies, PO Box 673, Belden Station, Norwalk, Connecticut 06852, USA

Prem Das: Mishakai Center for the Study of Shamanism, PO Box 844, Covelo, California 95428, USA

Sacraments Multidisciplinary Association for Psychedelic Studies, 2105 Robinson Avenue, Sarasota, Florida 34232, USA

Esoteric Order of Dagon, PO Box 5204, Eugene, Oregon 97405, USA

Publications *Shaman's Drum*, Box 2636, Berkeley, California 94702, USA

Magical Blend, PO Box 11303, San Francisco, California 94101-9950, USA

Selected Bibliography

Andrews, L.,   *Medicine Woman*, Harper & Row, San Francisco, 1981

Bardon, F.,   *The Practice of Magical Evocation*, Rudolf Pravica, Graz, 1967

Blacker, C.,   *The Catalpa Bow*, Allen & Unwin, London 1975

Butler, W.,   *The Magician, his Training and Work*, Aquarian Press, London, 1964

Case, P.,   *The Tarot*, Macoy Publishing Co., New York 1948

Castaneda, C.,   *The Teachings of Don Juan*, University of California Press, Berkeley, 1968
                    A Separate Reality, Simon & Schuster, New York, 1971
                    A Journey to Ixtlan, Simon & Schuster, New York, 1971
                    Tales of Power, Simon & Schuster, New York, 1974
                    The Second Ring of Power, Simon & Schuster, New York, 1976
                    The Eagle's Gift, Simon & Schuster, New York, 1981

Chevalier, G.,   *The Sacred Magician*, Paladin, London, 1976

Court de Gebelin.   *Le Monde Primitif*, Paris, 1775-84 (nine vols.)

Crowley, A.,   *Magick in Theory and Practice*, Routledge & Kegan Paul, London 1973

	The Book of Thoth, Weiser, New York, 1969
	The Vision and the Voice, Sangreal Foundation, Dallas, 1972
Drury, N.,	*The Path of the Chameleon*, Spearman, London, 1973
	Don Juan, Mescalito and Modern Magic, Routledge & Kegan Paul, London 1978
	Inner Visions, Routledge & Kegan Paul, London, 1979
	The Shaman and the Magician, Routledge & Kegan Paul, London 1982
Drury, N., and Skinner, S.,	*The Search for Abraxas*, Spearman, London, 1972
Eliade, M.,	*Shamanism*, Princeton University Press, 1972
Elkin, A.P.,	*Aboriginal Men of High Degree*, University of Queensland Press, 1977
Fortune, D.,	*The Mystical Qabalah*, Benn, London, 1966
Grant, K.,	*The Magical Revival*, Muller, London, 1972
	Images and Oracles of Austin Osman Spare, Muller, London, 1975
Grant, R.M.,	*Gnosticism: an Anthology*, Collins, London, 1961
Grof, S.,	*Realms of the Human Unconscious*, Dutton, New York, 1976
Halifax, J.,	*Shamanic Voices*, Dutton, New York, 1979
	Shaman, Crossroad, New York, 1982
Harner, M.,	*Hallucinogens and Shamanism*, Oxford University Press, New York, 1973
	The Way of the Shaman, Harper & Row, San Fancisco, 1980
Hesse, H.,	*Demian*, Peter Owen, London, 1960
Hillman, J.,	*Revisioning Psychology*, Harper & Row, New York, 1975

Howe, E.,	*The Magicians of the Golden Dawn*, Routledge & Kegan Paul, London 1972
Jung, C.G.,	*Memories, Dreams, Reflections*, Collins, London, 1967
	Septem Sermones ad Mortuos, Stuart & Watkins, London, 1967
King, F.,	*Astral Projection, Magic and Alchemy*, Spearman, London, 1971
King, F., & Skinner, S.,	*Techniques of High Magic*, C.W. Daniel, London, 1976
Knight, G.,	*A Practical Guide to Qabalistic Symbolism*, Helios, Cheltenham, 1965
Larsen, S.,	*The Shaman's Doorway*, Harper & Row, New York, 1976
Lilly, J.,	*The Centre of the Cyclone*, Calder & Boyars, London, 1972
	Simulations of God, Bantam, New York, 1975
	The Scientist, Lippincott, Philadelphia, 1978
Mathers, S.L.,	*The Kabbalah Unveiled*, George Redway, London, 1887
Masters, R., & Houston, J.,	*Mind Games*, Turnstone, London, 1973
	Varieties of Psychedelic Experience, Holt Reinhart & Winston, New York, 1966
	Psychedelic Art, Grove Press, New York, 1968
Masters, R.,	'The Way of the Five Bodies' *Dromenon* Journal, Vol III No. 2. Spring, 1981
Pagels, E.,	*The Gnostic Gospels*, Weidenfeld & Nicolson, London, 1980
Regardie, I.,	*The Tree of Life*, Rider, London 1932; republished by Weiser, New York, 1973
	The Golden Dawn, (4 vols.) Aries Press, Chicago, 1937-40; republished by Llewellyn, Minnesota, 1970

Robinson, J.M.,   *The Nag Hammadi Library*, Harper and Row, San Francisco 1977

Saint-   *The Most Holy Trinosophia*, Philosophers Press,
Germain, C.,   Los Angeles, 1949

Scholem, G.,   *Major Trends in Jewish Mysticism*, Schocken, New York 1961

Spare, A.,   *The Focus of Life*, Askin Press, London, 1976
                  The Book of Pleasure, 93 Publishing, Montreal, 1975
                  A Book of Satyrs, Co-operative Printing Co., London, 1907
                  The Starlit Mire, John Lane, London, 1911

Tarnas, R.,   'Ketamine', private paper, Esalen Institute, 1974

Tart, C.,   *Altered States of Consciousness*, Wiley, New York, 1969
                  Transpersonal Psychologies, Harper & Row, New York, 1975

Watkins, M.,   *Waking Dreams*, Gordon & Breach, New York, 1976

Waite, A.E.,   *The Pictorial Key to the Tarot*, Weiser, New York, 1963

Wilby, B.,   *New Dimensions Red Book*, Helios, Cheltenham, 1968

Yeats, W.B.,   *Mythologies*, Macmillan, London, 1959